MY AMERICA

AN OWNER'S GUIDE

BY WILLIAM E. WHITE

ILLUSTRATIONS BY CS JENNINGS

Colonial Williamsburg
The Colonial Williamsburg Foundation
Williamsburg, Virginia

ACKNOWLEDGMENTS

I was fortunate to collaborate with Michael Hartoonian and Richard Van Scotter on *The Idea of America: How Values Shaped Our Republic and Hold the Key to Our Future*, published in 2013. The ideas we explored in that book, especially about the Great Debate and value tensions, had a profound impact on my life and my teaching and on this book, *My America*.

© 2017 by The Colonial Williamsburg Foundation
All rights reserved. Published 2017.

30 29 28 27 26 25 24 23 22 21 20 19 18 17   1 2 3 4 5

Library of Congress Cataloging-in-Publication Data
Names: White, William E. (William Edward), 1953- author. | Jennings, C.S. illustrator.
Title: My America : an owner's guide / by William E. White ; illustrated by CS Jennings.
Description: Williamsburg, Virginia : The Colonial Williamsburg Foundation, 2017.
Identifiers: LCCN 2016037433 | ISBN 9780879352882 (paperback : alkaline paper)
Subjects: LCSH: United States--History--Philosophy. | United States--Politics and government--Philosophy. | Social values--United States--History. | Difference (Psychology)--Political aspects--United States--History. | National characteristics, American--History.
Classification: LCC E175.9 .W46 2017 | DDC 973.01--dc23 LC record available at https://lccn.loc.gov/2016037433

Designed by Shanin Glenn

Colonial Williamsburg is a registered trade name of
The Colonial Williamsburg Foundation, a not-for-profit
educational institution.

The Colonial Williamsburg Foundation
PO Box 1776
Williamsburg, VA 23187-1776
history.org

Printed in the United States of America

TABLE OF CONTENTS

INTRODUCTION .... PAGE 5
WE THE PEOPLE

CHAPTER 1 .... PAGE 19
POLITICIANS
UNITY AND DIVERSITY

CHAPTER 2 .... PAGE 47
PROTESTING
LAW AND ETHICS

CHAPTER 3 .... PAGE 79
GOING TO SCHOOL
COMMON WEALTH AND PRIVATE WEALTH

CHAPTER 4 .... PAGE 109
THE AMERICAN DREAM
FREEDOM AND EQUALITY

CONCLUSION .... PAGE 141
OUR AMERICA

INTRODUCTION: WE THE PEOPLE

THE AMERICAN CONVERSATION

This book is about how America works. Yes, we have a constitution, but the Constitution says how our national government works. Is the government actually America? Or is America the people?

That's actually how the Constitution starts, right? "We the People of the United States, in Order to form a more perfect Union." That one part of one sentence tells us a whole lot. You see, the American people were the ones who set up the government. It wasn't a ruler. It wasn't some smart person somewhere saying, "OK, this I how it's going to be." "We the People" had a big conversation about the kind of government we wanted to have. We actually debated with each other about what was the best system.

We tried out one government and decided it wasn't the right one. That was under the Articles of Confederation. The Continental Congress passed the Articles in 1777, though it took until 1781 for all the states to ratify, or approve, that form of government. Governing under the Articles did not go all that well: There was only the Congress, not the three branches of government like we have now. Under the Articles, the states had a hard time supporting the Revolutionary War army. And there was no way for the states to solve important problems. By 1787, many Americans were frustrated. The states sent delegates to meet at the Constitutional Convention to see what could be done. They made a new plan for government and created a new document—our Constitution. That Constitution went to every state. (Remember, there were only thirteen at the time.) And in every state the people debated whether or not it was a good form of government.

Not everyone was convinced, but in the end the people adopted the Constitution.

And that's how America works. Citizens—"We the People"—get together in communities all over the country and debate the issues. It's not always in formal meetings. It's amazing really. We talk with each other and express our opinions in so many different ways. And today, social media is expanding the discussion. Here are a few stories to help think about how these things happen.

> Coleen goes with her friends to the local recreation area pretty often. There's a great skate park there. Coleen is a big skateboarding fan. And she's pretty good at it.
>
> One day Coleen noticed this lady with a clipboard making notes. It seemed kind of weird. The lady had on a badge with the city's logo. The badge said her name was Angela. Coleen's just a naturally curious kind of person, so she decided to find out what was up.
>
> "You spying on us?" Coleen asked. Great way to start a conversation, right? Angela chuckled and said, "Yep."
>
> That caught Coleen off guard. "What do you mean you're spying on us?" she said a bit too defensively.
>
> "Well," said Angela, "I come out here all the time to see how people are using the facility."
>
> "Oh? Why?"

"I'm Angela by the way." She stuck her hand out, and Coleen shook it. "Here's the deal. I work for the city's Parks and Recreation Department. Every year we have to figure out the best way to spend our budget. So I come out and count the cars in the parking lot to help figure out which of our recreation areas is most popular. I look around and see what facilities are getting used the most. And I talk with the people using the park to find out what they like and don't like. After all, you are the citizens of the city. We're spending your tax money."

Coleen sort of cocked her head to the side and propped her skateboard against her leg. "I like the skate park—a lot."

"I can see that," Angela responded. "In fact, I've noticed that you and your friends are out here often. You know, this skate park is so popular we're thinking about expanding it."

"That's great! And you got all that just from watching?" Seeing a chance to make a pitch, Coleen quickly added, "You know, it would be cool to have a stair and a flat rail."

"Sure," chuckled Angela. "When people use the programs and services we provide, it's like they are voting. We watch pretty carefully. If people don't use a program or service, we close it down and put the money behind something people want to do. Or, if people really like something like this skate park, we figure out how to give it more resources."

Just think about all the places your family goes and the things you do. You drive on streets, go to the library, go to parks, use local sports facilities, go to school, use services like police and fire departments, send and receive mail. Those are just some of the public services in your community. The way you use those services, your comments, and your complaints are all part of a community discussion. It might seem small or insignificant, but you are expressing yourself every time you use public services and facilities. The same kind of thing happens with businesses and private organizations in your community.

> Jeremy just got diagnosed with type 1 diabetes. It stinks big time. And so Jeremy's learning to pay attention to his body and learn what it feels like when his blood sugar is too high or too low. He's working really hard to get his blood sugar regulated. The biggest pain is that you have to pay attention to it all the time. And that includes how you eat.
>
> Jeremy's whole family has been helping by watching their diet. And Jeremy's been going to the grocery store with his mom. Together they've been planning meals and learning about foods and nutrition. But Jeremy's been noticing something else as well.
>
> "Mom, I've only been coming to the grocery store with you for the last few months, but it seems to me like the store has been changing," Jeremy observed.
>
> "How do you mean?" his mom responded.
>
> "Well, look at the fruits and vegetables section. It seems like they have changed the way they display fruits and vegetables. And the section over there with organic foods is new, isn't it?"

"You're right," Jeremy's mom replied. "I guess the grocer is paying attention to the customers."

"What?"

"They're paying attention to the customers. When we come to the store and buy things, it's kind of like voting. If we buy lots of processed food, canned goods, or junk food, then the grocer stocks more of those things because they sell. But it looks like a lot of people are like us. They're buying more fresh fruits and vegetables."

"So the grocery store stocks more fresh fruit and vegetables because they sell?"

Jeremy's mom smiled, "If they want to stay in business."

"I just figured that some big company somewhere told the grocery store what to sell," Jeremy said.

"Actually, businesses don't survive if they don't meet the needs of their customers. We vote every day with the things we buy and the things we don't buy. So it's important to be an educated buyer. Make sure you know what you're getting."

"Buy more cookies!"

Jeremy's mom laughed and shook her head.

Other people, groups, and organizations even notice how we act. The things we do—or don't do—can make a difference.

There's a great area downtown. It has a bookstore, a couple of good places to get burgers and wings, and a movie theater with a big fountain out front. Scott and his friends like to meet there when the weather is nice. It's a cool place just to hang out and talk.

Maybe sometimes things get a bit rowdy. Like last week when this raucous game of tag got started and Jenny Harper chased him through the fountain. So maybe that was a bit wild, but it was fun. Some older people turned up their noses and huffed off, but what's the big deal, right?

This week, while Scott and his friends were hanging out, a policeman walked up.

"You kids need to move along," he said. His voice sounded firm, but not in a you-better-do-what-I-say-right-now kind of way, so Scott figured he could ask a question.

"Yes, sir," Scott said. "Did we do something wrong?"

"No, you're not in trouble. But the business owners here in this block have asked the city to make sure teenagers don't hang out around the fountain."

"We always hang out here. We just talk and stuff."

"Well, the way I understand it, some teenagers were out here last week being disruptive, running through the fountain, and bothering people. Apparently some people complained to the business owners and said they would stop coming down here to spend money. So the business owners called the city, the city called the chief of police, and the chief told me to come down here and make sure you teenagers don't hang out around the fountain. Sorry. Just doing my job."

"We weren't hurting anyone."

The cop smiled. "So you guys were the ones running through the fountain?"

"Well..."

"It's OK. But remember that people are watching. The way you act and the things you do—even if they seem harmless—can have consequences. People talk. Especially when they're not happy. So come on, kids, move along now."

Everything we do—from the conversations we have to the things we buy, the places we go, the way we act—are all part of a great big democratic conversation. It's always going on. What's really crazy is that most Americans don't pay very much attention to it. They think the only important conversations are the ones that politicians have in the halls of Congress or the White House. But, actually, those higher-up conversations don't happen in our country until after we've had a lot of local conversations.

"We the People" are the foundation of this really important conversation. If an issue is important to us, it becomes part of our conversation. Other people join in that conversation, and when it gets large enough, the people in community organizations and local, state, and federal government start to pay attention. In America, our businesses, institutions, and government respond to the people. When they don't, more people join in the discussion and turn up the volume so they will hear.

So we have this big conversation going on all the time because "We the People" are the ones who are shaping our community and deciding what we want to accomplish.

HISTORY IS THE KEY.

There is no rule book for how this conversation works. It's just something that has slowly taken shape over time. One of the best ways to see how it works is to look back at American history. That's where you can see groups of Americans at work shaping the country for themselves and for the next generation. You can see how they puzzled it out, see their mistakes, look at how they worked well together, and see how they disagreed and fought with each other.

When you look at our history, you also see that being a citizen is hard work. It's a messy job. Sometimes there are winners and losers. Sometimes we pull together and everyone wins. Sometimes things seem to fall apart, and everyone gets hurt. You realize pretty quickly that the citizens who did the work of creating and shaping this nation were everyday people just like you and me. We are good and bad, generous and greedy, hardworking and lazy, forgiving and vengeful. We are not perfect. We make mistakes. We do remarkable things. We are human beings.

The other thing you realize is that we work on the same issues over and over again because the answers one generation came up with don't necessarily work for the next generations. The first generation of Americans talked about how to defend the country. Guess what, we're still talking about the issue of military defense today. The circumstances have changed. We don't need the same type of defense they needed in 1776. We have to come up with our own answer to the problem of defending the nation. You name it—education, race, immigration, civil rights, violence in our communities, political parties, technology—every generation of Americans has tackled the issues important to them.

THE GREAT DEBATE

This book is going to look at this big conversation, this "Great Debate." It is the long-running formal and informal exchange of ideas that Americans have had all through our history. It continues today.

We are going to look at the Great Debate in a special way. When Americans have this debate, they are always thinking about eight treasured American values. A value is a belief that a whole group—in this case Americans—agree on. These are ideas that are important to every American. And we need to think about these values in pairs because they push and pull on each other.

UNITY AND DIVERSITY

We are one nation, and the American people are like a family. You might not like your little sister all that much, but when someone outside the family says something bad about your sister, you get mad. It's OK for you to tease her but not for some stranger to do it. Americans are pretty much the same way. We are proud of being American. We can pull together as one nation.

But we know we are not all the same. We actually like the fact that individuals are different. We celebrate all the different cultures that make up our country. We talk about Italian Americans, Native Americans, African Americans, Chinese Americans. We are of many different religions. We are northerners, southerners, midwesterners, westerners. Some enjoy baseball, others football, soccer, or another sport. You get the picture. We are not all the same.

That's one of the tensions we will look at in this book. How unified do we need to be? How much can we celebrate our diversity? How do those two things work together?

PRIVATE WEALTH AND COMMON WEALTH

Americans like stuff. We are big consumers. We like our homes and TV sets and cell phones and video games. Who doesn't like cool stuff? You can think about all that stuff—that property—as private wealth. We believe that we have a right to property. We should be able to have whatever we can afford. And wealth is not necessarily physical things. An educated person has knowledge. That's private wealth. A religious person has faith. That's private wealth. Sometimes you can touch private wealth, and sometimes it enriches you in other ways.

At the same time, we all have to live together, and we have to sacrifice some things in order to live together. After all, the writers of the Declaration of Independence pledged to each other "our Lives, our Fortunes and our sacred Honor." They were willing to contribute all they had—all of their private wealth—in order to create a new country—a new common wealth—for all. We can see common wealth all around us. It's our government, our roads, our military, our hospitals, our places of worship. And there are things that are harder to see, but we feel them, like our liberty, our safety, and our welfare.

That's the second pair we will look at. How much private wealth can you have? And how much of that private wealth will you give up to help create common wealth? Does a strong common wealth help create more private wealth? Or does it just take away private wealth?

LAW AND ETHICS

We are a nation founded on law. The Constitution is, after all, a contract among the people, the states, and our national government. When we have disagreements, we go to court to settle them. When we need to build things like roads and schools, we pass a law. And we obey laws in order to keep our communities safe. But just because it's a law doesn't mean it's right.

After all, there have been laws that were not right—that were unethical. Sometimes we make laws that hurt people. African Americans were held in slavery for a long time after the Constitution was adopted. It was legal in many places. But it wasn't right. It wasn't ethical.

In the United States, we are always trying to make sure we balance our laws and our ethics.

That's the third pair we will look at. How do we make laws that are ethical? How do we fix it when our laws don't do the right thing? Are there times when we need to make unethical laws? Are there some things that are ethical—the right way to live—but we just can't express them as laws?

FREEDOM AND EQUALITY

Every American wants to be free. That's why we fought the American Revolution. Remember Patrick Henry's famous "Give me liberty, or give me death!" speech? We want as much individual freedom as we can have, but it just isn't possible to be completely free. Complete individual freedom would get out of hand. Some people would end up doing things that hurt other people because they have the power to do it. We all know a bully.

Equality is the way we limit our individual freedom. We all want equal opportunity to be free. It helps us keep everything fair—our laws, our businesses, our communities, even our relationships with other people. We try, for example, to make sure everyone has an equal opportunity to get an education. Education is important, so it isn't fair if some people receive an education and others do not have that same opportunity.

That doesn't mean that we are all the same. We don't want to be just like everybody else. And we continue to try to figure out a way to have the most individual freedom and the most equality at the same time. We've been searching for that since the days before the Revolution.

So there's the last pair. How much individual freedom can we have and still be comfortable that we all have equality? And what happens if we have too much equality? Does that mean we have to go along with the group all the time? How will that limit my individual freedom to do what I want to do?

WHAT'S YOUR PLAN?

The Great Debate, involving these four pairs of values, is going on every day in America in every community in the nation. It has been going on all throughout our history. You can actually go back and look at the conversations we've had in the past. It helps you understand how and why we are having that same debate today.

So we're going to take a look at four conversations that have been going on since before the American Revolution and see how this Great Debate has worked. But more importantly, we're also going to think about how this Great Debate still works today and what kind of role you have in the future of your community, your state, and the nation.

WHAT ARE YOU GOING TO DO?

WHAT'S YOUR PLAN?

HOW ARE YOU GOING TO JOIN THE DEBATE?

YOU ARE, AFTER ALL, AN IMPORTANT PART OF "WE THE PEOPLE."

POLITICIANS

CHAPTER ONE

UNITY AND DIVERSITY

GEORGE HATED POLITICS.

Some say George Washington was our country's greatest statesman ever. George hated politics. He worried about bad politicians and political parties. In 1796, President Washington was tired. He had a right to be tired. He'd spent eight years (1775–1783) as commander in chief of America's first army. Then he was the first president of the United States for eight years (1789–1797). And the whole time he worked with politicians.

Just before Washington retired, he wrote a letter to the nation—Washington's Farewell Address. He told the American people what he hoped for the future of America. Washington saw a lot of promise, and a bunch of problems. Political parties were one of the things he worried about. Political parties, he feared, would get out of hand. Before too long, Washington said, the politicians and political parties would be manipulating each other and the people. Today we call that partisan politics. Washington called it a "fire" that could destroy the nation.

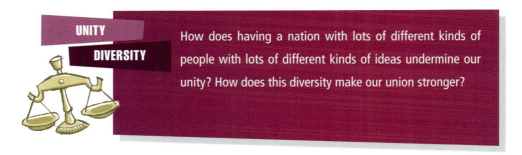

UNITY / DIVERSITY

How does having a nation with lots of different kinds of people with lots of different kinds of ideas undermine our unity? How does this diversity make our union stronger?

But Washington was a dreamer. Americans have always disagreed with each other, and political parties are one way we express our differences. Americans are always walking in the "fire." So far it hasn't destroyed us. Maybe it makes us stronger. What do you think?

IF IT'S A PARTY AND POLITICAL, IS IT FUN?

Alexis de Tocqueville was a Frenchman who visited America in the 1830s. We were still a very new country. Europeans were interested in how things worked over here. So Alexis wrote down his thoughts about America. One thing he noticed was that we join together in groups to learn and debate. A historian many years later said that de Tocqueville saw Americans as a "nation of joiners."

In 1830 Americans gathered in meeting halls, taverns, churches, and homes to talk things through. Today we gather online. But in a lot of ways it's the same thing. We express ourselves. What do we like? What do we hate? And we usually gather with people who like and hate the same stuff.

Politics is one of the places where the American people divide. We divide as we discuss how to solve the problems in front of us. That's how we get political parties—that thing that George hated. We're all Americans—that's unity. And, at the very same time, we see different ways to solve our problems—that's diversity.

It's always been that way. In the 1790s, during George Washington's presidency, Americans argued about the future of the country. It took almost ten years, but by 1800 they had formed into two different parties. The parties were called Federalist and Democratic Republican.

Politics is the debate—the conversation—among citizens about our community and government. We participate in politics whenever we discuss things related to our community and government, like schools, parks, laws, and community programs.

Politicians work in government. Some are elected. Some volunteer. Some are appointed or hired. We find politicians in school government, teams, and other organizations. And, of course, there are politicians in local, state, and federal government.

Some politicians do a great job. When they do—when they draw citizens together and help us be the best we can be—we honor them and call them statesmen or stateswomen. They are skilled and respected political leaders. There are lots of examples in our history. George Washington was a statesman. So was Martin Luther King Jr. (Remember, political leaders are not necessarily elected leaders.) Retired U.S. Supreme Court justice Sandra Day O'Connor is a stateswoman.

Jot down some other statesmen and stateswomen. Remember, these do not have to be national figures. You might find a statesman in your school or your community.

We sometimes use the word "politician" to describe someone devious who manipulates others. That's why you often see people roll their eyes when they use the word "politician."

But good and bad, politicians are very important to the American debate—the discussion we are always having about our values and how we should build a future together.

CRUMMY FEDERALISTS, LOUSY DEMOCRATIC REPUBLICANS

Federalists believed in a strong federal government. They wanted the federal government to take charge of the country. For the most part, Democratic Republicans believed that state and local governments were more important than the national government. After all, more citizens participate directly in local and state governments.

As the election of 1800 neared, these two parties went at each other big time. Just imagine what the Twitter feed between Federalists and Democratic Republicans would have looked like.

POTUS stands for "president of the United States."

John Adams: Federalist and one-term POTUS, 1797–1801. Had been friends with Jefferson.

Jacobin: Radical French revolutionaries who executed the king and queen of France (and many others). Federalists labeled Democratic Republicans as radicals too because Democratic Republicans thought the French Revolution was a good thing and favored an alliance with the French.

In France, **mobs** called for the execution of political prisoners. Thousands were beheaded by guillotine. Could a mob do the same thing in Washington, D.C., Philadelphia, or New York? Federalists worried that's what would happen if the Democratic Republicans took over.

Thomas Jefferson: Democratic Republican, secretary of state under George Washington, and John Adams's vice president. (That was a problem! When did they fix the Constitution to make sure the president and vice president come from the same party? 1804. It's the Twelfth Amendment to the Constitution.)

Remember, the American people fought the Revolution to get away from King George III of Great Britain. To call someone **"king"** was a big insult.

The Federalists' Alien and Sedition Acts (1798) gave the federal government power to **arrest** "dangerous" foreigners as well as citizens who criticized the U.S. government.

William Linn was a New York minister who warned that Jefferson would "destroy religion, introduce immorality, and loosen all the bonds of society."

Jefferson's support for religious freedom and some of his writings led Federalists to charge that he was an **atheist** (someone who does not believe in God). Even today, historians disagree about whether Jefferson was a Christian or an atheist or neither.

David Tappan was head of Harvard Divinity School in Massachusetts.

Federalists warned that Democratic Republicans would promise not to interfere with religion but, as soon as they were elected, would close churches and take away Bibles.

Baptist and other evangelicals believed that government should not regulate a person's **religion**.

Gowan Pamphlet was an enslaved African American Baptist preacher in Williamsburg, Virginia. By 1781 his congregation had upwards of two hundred members. Pamphlet gained his freedom in 1793.

FREEDOM/EQUALITY

Should we all have the same **religion**? In a way, that would make us all equal—or all the same. Or should we have the freedom to practice any religion, even no religion?

Several Democratic Republicans were arrested and charged for speaking out against the Federalist administration.

Jefferson hates religion! He'll take your Bibles away.
William Linn @preacherbill

TJ doesn't hate religion! But he won't force me to be a Puritan. I'm a Baptist. NO STATE RELIGION!
Gowan Pamphlet @VABaptist

Jefferson is an atheist! Democratic Republicans will destroy all religion. Woe is America!
David Tappan @HarvardReligionProf

Don't tread on me!!! Jefferson for religious freedom!
Gowan Pamphlet @VABaptist

Democratic Republicans will do or say anything to get power. #nomorals #voteAdams
John Adams @realjohna

King Adams throws you in jail if you speak against him. Protect #freespeech #voteJefferson
Thomas Jefferson @TJtheDR

@TJtheDR You lie! I am only protecting the nation!
John Adams @realjohna

Federalist Alien and Sedition Acts imprison Americans who disagree with John Adams. Protect #freespeech #voteJefferson
Thomas Jefferson @TJtheDR

CHAPTER 1: POLITICIANS

France and Great Britain were at war. Federalists charged that Democratic Republicans supported French agents who tried to get the American people to support France against Great Britain.

> Jefferson lets French spies into America trying to get us to go to war against Great Britain.
> **John Adams** @realjohna

> Adams forgets why we fought the Revolution. #freedom #noKingGeorge
> **Thomas Jefferson** @TJtheDR

Federalists supported Great Britain in the war between Britain and France.

Alexander Hamilton was a New York businessman and lawyer and leading Federalist politician. He served as President Washington's secretary of the treasury, where he clashed with Secretary of State Jefferson. No love lost there.

> Great Britain is our best trading partner. Jefferson will destroy our economy by taking up with the French.
> **Alexander Hamilton** @Federalist1

> @Federalist1 and his money friends are getting rich by destroying American #freedom.
> **Thomas Jefferson** @TJtheDR

Federalists wanted to rebuild **trade between Britain** and her former American colonies. Democratic Republicans worried that King George just wanted to get his colonies back.

> Strong banks and good trade with Great Britain benefit every American.
> **Alexander Hamilton** @Federalist1

> Banks and merchants suck the lifeblood from farmers. Support Main St. not Wall St. #agriculturerules #freedom #voteJefferson
> **Thomas Jefferson** @TJtheDR

Federalists wanted to build strong banks and a system of trade with Great Britain. Democratic Republicans felt these policies hurt farmers.

Some Northern states had taken steps to begin abolishing slavery. Northern Federalists criticized Southern **slaveholders** who betrayed the ideals of the American Revolution. Remember, the Declaration of Independence states that "all men are created equal."

> Jefferson the farmer? Jefferson the slave owner, you mean. "All men are created equal"? Jefferson and slavery betray the Revolution. #noslavery #freedom #freeman
> **John Adams** @realjohna

> Cannot end slavery yet.
> **Thomas Jefferson** @TJtheDR

LAW/ETHICS
In those days it was legal to own a slave, but was it right? Was it ethical? What does the Declaration of Independence say?

> @TJtheDR I hate you.
> **John Adams** @realjohna

> @realjohna You are such a little man.
> **Thomas Jefferson** @TJtheDR

Tempers ran high. During the election of 1800, Adams and Jefferson stopped talking to each other. They would not talk to each other again until 1811.

Lots of yelling. Not much listening. That's one thing about political campaigns that has not changed much in two hundred years. It's just that the political parties have different names. It started with Federalists and Democratic Republicans. Then it was Whigs and Democrats. Today it's Republicans and Democrats. George Washington may have hated political parties, but throughout our history Americans have found political parties to be important.

Jefferson won the election of 1800. It was the first time that the United States peaceably passed control of government from one political party to another—from Federalists to Democratic Republicans. In his inaugural address, Jefferson recalled how bitterly the parties fought during the campaign. "But," he said, "every difference of opinion is not a difference of principle. We have called by different names brethren of the same principle. We are all republicans: we are all federalists." He also reminded those listening that the United States was "the world's best hope."

Americans have very different ideas about the course our government should take, and we organize in groups and parties to support the ideas we believe in. We are diverse. And we are not bashful about telling other people that we are right and they are wrong. At the same time, we are one people—the American people. We believe in democracy. We believe that by working together—debating the issues—we can build a better world. Always remember that our unity gives hope to the American people and to the world.

THE PARTY THAT KNOWS NOTHING

Are you an American? How do you know? Who is an American? Who is not? Is it possible that some of the people living in the United States are just not American enough?

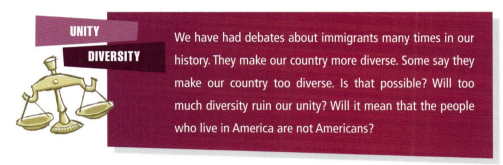

UNITY
DIVERSITY

We have had debates about immigrants many times in our history. They make our country more diverse. Some say they make our country too diverse. Is that possible? Will too much diversity ruin our unity? Will it mean that the people who live in America are not Americans?

This can be an uncomfortable conversation. Many times, discussing citizenship becomes an attack on an ethnic or minority group.

Politicians and political parties sometimes attack other groups. It's called *demagoguery.* That's when a person or group says that they are the good guys, the insiders, the in-group and all of the country's problems are caused by another person or group who is different from them. The "outsiders" are often immigrants, people of color, or people with a different religion. That was the case in the 1850s.

America was changing in the 1840s and 1850s. The founding generation had passed away. John Adams and Thomas Jefferson died in 1826. James Madison, father of the Constitution, died in 1836. And America was growing. California became the thirty-first state in 1850. Immigrants were pouring into the country. Fast.

In the 1820s, fewer than 150,000 immigrants arrived in the United States. Mostly they came from Great Britain. In the 1840s, 1.7 million

immigrants arrived. These immigrants were mostly from Germany and Ireland. Germans were fleeing political wars and revolutions at home. When they arrived in America, they still spoke German and not English. Irish immigrants were fleeing famine and poverty. The Irish were mostly Catholics, and at the time the United States was mostly a Protestant nation. Many Americans worried that these immigrants would not fit in. They worried that Germans and Irish would change America.

New politicians and political groups organized, believing that the only way to save America—to save what the founding generation had created—was to keep the foreigners out. Can you imagine what it was like? Here's just one story to give you an idea.

SECRET ORDER, SECRET OATH

Benjamin remembered how angry he was that morning. He and two friends, Charlie and Will, had walked down to the Cincinnati docks, on the Ohio River. They were looking for some work.

In Cincinnati there was always a steamboat tied up at the landing. He and his friends were paid fair wages for a good day's work around the docks. Then things started to change.

The Irish started coming around. It seemed like more and more of those Irishmen were working the docks. You could hardly understand a word they said even though they claimed to speak English, but it wasn't any good American English, that's for sure. Then the morning came when Benjamin and his friends went down to the docks and the boss told them there was no work.

"What do you mean no work?" demanded Will. "Looks to me like there's plenty of boats tied up here. There's plenty of men loading and unloading!"

"Why don't you have work for us?" Benjamin asked.

"I got Irish down here working now," the boss replied. "They work longer hours and at cheaper wages to boot."

Charlie was red in the face. "You gave them Irish my job? That's a job for an American, not some Irish Catholic devil!" Benjamin got a grip on Charlie's sleeve, just in case Charlie had it in mind to go after the boss. It wouldn't do any good to start a fight.

"Come on, Charlie. Let's go."

That was the day Benjamin started to notice how much things had changed. Walking down the streets of Cincinnati, he heard strange languages. Germans talking German to each other. The Irish and their strange English. And something Charlie told him was Norwegian. It wasn't bad enough that these foreigners were coming and taking work from him. They couldn't even be bothered to learn how to speak the language. What's wrong with them? "How long you figure before we gotta learn to speak German?" Charlie wanted to know.

Then there were the Irish—the Catholics. Benjamin had never known a Catholic. He grew up going to the Methodist meetinghouse with his parents. He knew some Baptists, and he even knew a few Presbyterians. He had heard some disturbing things about Catholics. He had heard that they worshipped a man over in Rome called the *pope*. These Catholics, he figured, were going to follow that pope's instructions. If the pope said, "Overthrow the American government," then these Irish were sure to rise up and do it.

And none of these foreigners knew anything about democracy, the responsibility of voting, and the Constitution of these United States. How could they? thought Benjamin. They were born and raised in Europe, where they still had kings and lords and such. Being an American citizen was too important to trust to these foreigners. They would ruin the country for sure. You needed to be raised an American to understand. Only an American could protect the Republic.

FREEDOM

EQUALITY

Do you have to be born in America to be equal? Do you have to grow up with American freedoms to understand them? Maybe foreigners are not ready for equality?

As Benjamin pondered these things and discussed them with friends, he found out that there were others who felt the same as he did. He discovered that these men were meeting together in a secret society. They called themselves Know-Nothings because when someone asked them about the activities of the party, they were supposed to answer, "I know nothing!" Know-Nothings were

planning how to protect the United States of America from all these foreigners. Benjamin decided it was his patriotic duty to help. That's how Benjamin came to be standing in the lamplight at the front of the meetinghouse on a cold March evening. He stood with a man, the examiner, in front of nearly a hundred other men.

"Are you a candidate for membership to our order?" asked the examiner.

"I am," Benjamin replied.

The examiner continued with firm voice and stern look: "You do solemnly promise, declare, and swear . . . before Almighty God, and these witnesses, that you will not divulge or make known to any person whatever, the nature of the questions I may ask you here, the names of the persons you may see here, or that you know that such an organization is going on as such, whether you become a member of our organization or not. Will you promise me this?"

"I will," came the reply.

"And that you will true and faithful answers give to all the questions I may ask you?"

"I will!" Everyone in the hall heard Benjamin deliver the promise in a strong, true, confident voice.

"Are you by religious faith a Roman Catholic?"

"No!" he declared. "I am not."

"Were you born in this country?"

"I was," the young man nodded.

"Were either of your parents?"

"My parents were born in America," Benjamin affirmed.

"Any of your grandparents?"

"Aye, sir, my grandparents are native born as well!" A murmur of approval rumbled through the audience.

"Were any of your ancestors in this country during the Revolutionary War?"

"My grandfather fought with General Washington at the Battle of Yorktown!" Benjamin puffed himself up with pride as he said it.

"Then as you swear all that to be true—Are you willing to use your influence to elect to all offices of honor, profit, or trust none but native-born citizens of America, of this country, in the exclusion of all foreigners, and to all Roman Catholics, whether they be of native or foreign birth, regardless of all party predilections whatever?"

LAW
ETHICS
Is it right to make a law saying only American-born people can run for office? Why? Do native-born citizens make the best, most ethical laws?

"I am!" And the other members of the group, known as the American Party or the Know-Nothings, applauded and cheered.

AMERICANS FIRST

That kind of scene was repeated in gatherings across the country. In the 1850s many Americans worried that immigrants—Germans and Irish Catholics in particular—were destroying the country.

The American Party (or Know-Nothings) met in Philadelphia during February 1856. They outlined their principles. The founding generation, after a "successful Revolutionary struggle," created the country and handed down to native-born Americans responsibility to protect "the liberties, the independence and the union of these States." The party pledged to protect "civil and religious liberties" and opposed "any union between Church and State." Most important, "Americans must rule America." Only "native-born citizens should be selected for all State, Federal, and municipal offices of government employment."

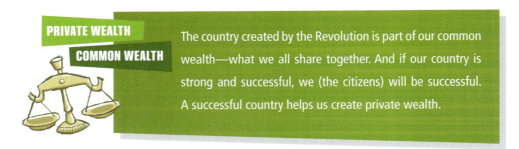

PRIVATE WEALTH / COMMON WEALTH The country created by the Revolution is part of our common wealth—what we all share together. And if our country is strong and successful, we (the citizens) will be successful. A successful country helps us create private wealth.

NO FOREIGNERS!

The Know-Nothing Party did not last very long, but the impact was real. It showed how many people across the country felt about people different from themselves, be they Native Americans, African Americans, or immigrants. By the 1850s most voting citizens of America decided that these "other people" were not really Americans.

Today Americans proudly display their German or Irish heritage. African Americans and Native Americans have struggled harder for recognition. Unfortunately, still today there are groups claiming that America is only for people of European heritage. And there are still groups today that want to keep immigrants out.

The issues raised by immigration are a regular part of our political discussion. Do you ever wonder how we can come from so many different places, backgrounds, religions, and ethnicities? We are so diverse. Yet still, we sometimes point at others and say that they don't belong, that they are not Americans.

IT'S RISKY.

Politicians don't spend all of their time bickering with each other. And they don't spend all of their time figuring out how to stick it to someone else (like in the case of the Know-Nothings and immigrants). Politicians will tell you that they got into politics because they want to help people, they want to do good things for the community, the state, and the nation. Politicians are like any other people—complicated. If you look back in our history, you see that politicians have done some amazing things. They often take risks to improve the world. Taking a risk is tricky. Sometimes you're successful. Sometimes you fail.

Teddy Roosevelt was not supposed to be president of the United States. He was elected vice president on the 1900 Republican ticket with President William McKinley. Roosevelt had been the governor of New York, but as governor he frustrated the state Republican Party politicians. He wanted to improve the way government worked, and the party politicians liked things just as they were, thank you very much. To get Roosevelt out of the way, they managed to get him nominated as McKinley's running mate. Vice presidents are busier and more involved today, but in 1900 it was pretty much a do-nothing kind of job. The idea was that, once Roosevelt was elected vice president, he would be out of everybody's way.

But, on September 6, 1901, an anarchist named Leon Czolgosz shot President McKinley. An anarchist believes in complete individual freedom and is against just about all forms of government. President McKinley died eight days later on September 14. And that's how Teddy Roosevelt became president of the United States.

Roosevelt became president at a time when African Americans faced severe discrimination. At the end of the Civil War, three amendments to the Constitution promised a new era for African Americans. The Thirteenth Amendment abolished slavery in the United States. The Fourteenth Amendment guaranteed equal protection to all citizens. And the Fifteenth Amendment said that you could not deny the right to vote to any citizen based on race, color, or "previous condition of servitude."

Still, in the thirty years following the Civil War, white Americans found ways to keep African Americans from being equal citizens.

It was a system of what became known as Jim Crow laws—laws that restricted the freedoms of African Americans. Jim Crow laws said African Americans couldn't use the same waiting room in the train terminal or ride in the same train car as whites. African Americans were not allowed to use the same bathroom or water fountain. As they were written, the laws called only for separate facilities. But do you know what really happened? African Americans almost always received second-rate facilities and services. Other Jim Crow laws allowed businesses to refuse to serve African Americans in restaurants and stores. These laws were passed and enforced in states across the country. Even the U.S. Supreme Court agreed that Jim Crow laws were legal. The decision in the case of *Plessy v. Ferguson* confirmed that the segregation and separate treatment of African American citizens was constitutional. The Ku Klux Klan and other white supremacist groups were very active. In communities across America, African Americans were discouraged from voting and participating in politics. Often, African Americans faced violence designed to "keep them in their place."

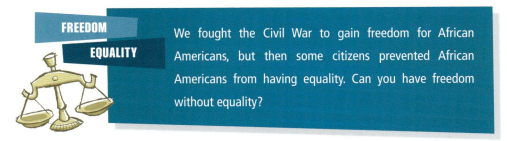

FREEDOM
EQUALITY

We fought the Civil War to gain freedom for African Americans, but then some citizens prevented African Americans from having equality. Can you have freedom without equality?

In the midst of all this racism, Teddy Roosevelt invited an African American to dine with him and his family. No big deal, right? Wrong.

TEDDY TAKES A CHANCE.

Teddy Roosevelt was a progressive. That's what you called someone in 1900 who wanted to see change. What kind of change? Better government for one thing. Roosevelt wanted everyday Americans to have a better life. He wanted America to be fairer for everyone. How do you change things? Teddy Roosevelt believed that individuals changed things.

PRIVATE WEALTH
COMMON WEALTH

An individual's beliefs are part of private wealth. But what happens when an individual's beliefs shock the way the whole community believes? A single person can rock the foundation of our common wealth.

A lot of things that presidents do are symbolic. Presidents cannot change the law, or the way people act, but they can do symbolic things that set examples. They can show the right kind of character.

Booker T. Washington headed the Tuskegee Institute in Alabama. He was a nationally recognized African American leader in 1900. But that's not how Washington began his life. He was born a slave in southwest Virginia in 1856. He was one of the thousands and thousands of African Americans whose life was profoundly affected by the Thirteenth, Fourteenth, and Fifteenth Amendments to the Constitution that ended slavery and recognized African American citizenship and civil rights. But by 1901, Washington and every other African American in the United States felt the oppression of Jim Crow.

It was very symbolic, then, when Teddy Roosevelt invited Booker T. Washington to dine at the White House in October 1901. The dinner included Mr. and Mrs. Roosevelt, four of their children, a family friend, and Booker T. Washington. We don't really know what was said that evening. Perhaps they discussed what they could do to improve race relations in America. It did not really matter what they said to each other because just having the dinner spoke volumes: It said that the president of the United States recognized that he represented all the citizens of the United States including African Americans.

The reaction from the black community was very positive. One man telegraphed to say the dinner was the "greatest step for the race in a generation." Another person hoped this was the "beginning of a new order." It "was a masterly stroke of statesmanship," declared still another man. But white Americans did not see it the same way.

> **JUDGE G. K. ANDERSON OF RICHMOND, VIRGINIA:**
>
> If Mr. Roosevelt wants to entertain negroes at his private table, he has the right to do so. There is no law against it. But he is, or ought to be, the Chief Magistrate of the whole people, and he occupies a house provided for his use by the whole nation. A decent regard for the opinions of a large part of the people . . . ought to have prevented his ill-advised action. The South is willing to accord the colored man all necessary rights and privileges, but social equality is one that is not only not necessary, but is hurtful to the negro, and never will be tolerated by the white people, north or south.

Is he really saying, if you're not white like me, you are not a full American?

> **THE *SCIMITAR*, A MEMPHIS, TENNESSEE, NEWSPAPER:**
>
> The most damnable outrage which has ever been perpetrated by any citizen of the United States was committed yesterday by the President when he invited a n----- to dine with him at the White House. . . .
>
> The President has rudely shattered any expectations that may have arisen from his announced intention to make the Republican party in the South respectable. He has closed the door to . . . southern white men.

And, yes, the newspaper printed the "n" word several times in this editorial just as plain as day. No doubt where the editor of the *Scimitar* of Memphis stood.

> **THE *COMMERCIAL APPEAL*, ANOTHER MEMPHIS, TENNESSEE, NEWSPAPER:**
>
> [America] is a white man's country. It will continue to be such as long as clean blood flows through the veins of white people. The negro.... is entitled to his rights under the law.... [but white] race supremacy precludes social equality.

A white man's country? Is that what America is?

> **U.S. SENATOR BENJAMIN R. TILLMAN OF SOUTH CAROLINA:**
>
> The action of President Roosevelt in entertaining that n----- will necessitate our killing a thousand n------ in the South before they learn their place again.

A U.S. senator quoted using the "n" word and threatening to kill African Americans! And make no mistake about it, African Americans *were* dying across America. Violence was used as a tool to suppress African Americans' equality. Today Tillman's comment would be shocking. No one was that surprised by it in 1901.

LAW
ETHICS

Don't we expect our leaders to be law abiding? Can you imagine a senator suggesting that we murder men and women? How important is it for our leaders to be ethical men and women?

It's hard to imagine today, but that was the reaction of many whites across the nation and in particular the South.

Although Teddy Roosevelt decided to wait for the storm to blow over, his belief was consistent with his action: "The only wise and honorable and Christian thing to do," Roosevelt wrote to a supporter, "is to treat each black man and each white man strictly on his merits as a man, giving him no more and no less than he shows himself worthy to have."

But the storm did not blow over. It was almost thirty years before another African American was invited to a social event at the White House.

BULLY PULPIT

President Roosevelt used the word *bully* a lot. When he called something "bully," he meant that it was wonderful or superb. During his presidency Roosevelt coined a new phrase: *bully pulpit.* It described using the office of president to push for important changes. After all, everybody listens to what the president says. But in the case of inviting Booker T. Washington to the White House, the bully pulpit did not work very well.

Or maybe it's just that Roosevelt gave up too easily? Maybe he should have invited Booker T. Washington and other African American leaders to come back to the White House. It may have been one way to make clear to the critics that, as far as he was concerned, they were wrong. What do you think?

Sometimes we stand up for a principle that is not popular, and we take some heat for it.

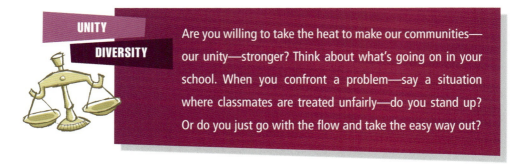

UNITY

DIVERSITY

Are you willing to take the heat to make our communities—our unity—stronger? Think about what's going on in your school. When you confront a problem—say a situation where classmates are treated unfairly—do you stand up? Or do you just go with the flow and take the easy way out?

In the case of a politician like Teddy Roosevelt, there can be some tough consequences. In 1901, newspapers were very important to politicians. The endorsement, or support, of newspapers helped get you elected. And newspapers were important to getting the support a president needed in Congress. Southern newspapers were pretty clear that they would not support Roosevelt going forward. Maybe Roosevelt felt like he had to cave in order to win the next election and get congressional support for other things he wanted to do.

Was it right for Roosevelt to cave on African American equality? Should he have done more—no matter what the consequences? All through the 1900s, African Americans pressured politicians for equality. Some of their political actions were met with violence. Some African Americans and their supporters were injured and even killed. But the push for political action continued. It continues today. And that is one major purpose for the Great Debate—making sure that all of us are part of the unity we call America, no matter how diverse our races, religions, beliefs.

WE'RE ALL POLITICIANS.

It's not just POTUS who has the bully pulpit. We are all citizens. In the United States of America, it's "We the People." We are all politicians. Every one of us should work to be a statesman or stateswoman.

That doesn't mean that every one of us will be a leader who solves a major world problem. But we can—each of us—work to make our community, state, and nation a better place for us all. That's what stateswomen and statesmen do. That's what citizens do. We work every day to make our home, our school, our place of work, our community, our state, our nation a better place, a freer place, a place that really does have "liberty and justice for all."

We have a lot of different ideas, though, on how to do that. We are very different—diverse. And that's a good thing in the end. We all have different life experiences. What works for westerners might not work for easterners. What's good for one group might frighten others. A policy might be good for the boss, but workers might not agree. Just think about how many different ways you can describe yourself. Your combination of life experiences is different from anyone else's.

America is a place where each of us can bring our unique experience and participate in the debate—the conversation about how we will build our future together. All those different experiences make the decisions better in the end. Remember though, it's politics. Politics is messy. Sometimes it makes us feel divided. Sometimes it causes us to turn on each other. Sometimes we take a risk and fail. It can take a lot of time to be successful. It can be hard to see and do the best thing, the right thing.

BE A CITIZEN, BE A STATESMAN.

What can you do to be a citizen? Get involved. Your point of view matters. Make a list. What are the things you care about? What are the things you're passionate about? Now think about the future of those things. How can you help make that future possible?

You're already doing the work of a citizen.

Just remember there are a lot of different ways to look at an issue,

the thing you're passionate about. But once you get involved, you have a chance to tell others about your opinions. You will, no doubt, find some people who think differently than you. That's OK. It's part of the diversity that makes America so strong.

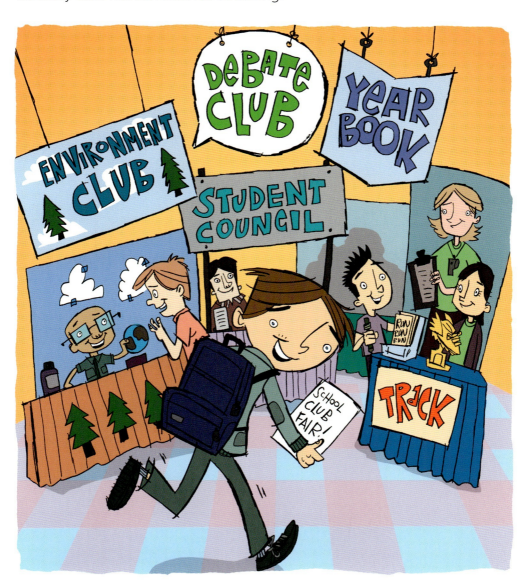

If you're part of the political discussion, you'll have a chance to convince others that your way of solving a problem or helping the community is the right way. More importantly, you just might discover that other people have a way to improve on your idea. You will discover that the conversation—the debate—also brings people together. It creates unity.

Be a stateswoman or statesman. Help draw citizens in your community together. Help those diverse people all around you become the best. When Americans come together, we accomplish remarkable things. Being a citizen politician is hard work. Being an American is hard work. But it's oh so worth it.

CHAPTER TWO: PROTESTING

LAW AND ETHICS

WHO'S THE SUBJECT?

In 1761 Thomas Jefferson was a student at the College of William and Mary in Williamsburg, Virginia. If you had asked him then about citizenship, Tom would have replied, "I'm a subject of King George!"

No, not like the person, place, or thing subject of a sentence. This is different.

By "subject," Tom would have meant that he was under the control, or authority, of King George. In Europe at the time, this was a pretty normal way of looking at government. It was based on an idea called "the divine right of kings." The idea was that God gave rights and privileges to a monarch (king or queen). The monarch then gave rights and privileges to the people he or she ruled. But don't forget: If a monarch can grant rights and privileges to people, a monarch can also take away rights and privileges.

There was representative government at the time. The British Parliament, for example, had a House of Lords (representing noblemen and the clergy) and a House of Commons (representing common people). But the king *allowed* his subjects to have a legislature. He gave permission. The people were still subjects of the monarch.

But there were some new ideas floating around that would change how people thought about government.

A group of thinkers came up with a different idea of how things worked. Their idea was that God granted rights and privileges to *people* and people chose the government. If the people could give rights to government, the people could also take away those rights. These new political ideas were part of what we call the *Enlightenment*.

WHO CARES ABOUT LIGHTS?

People in Europe had always thought they needed rulers. Then this Enlightenment idea popped up, and people started to go, "Aha!" It's like that cartoon bubble with the lightbulb in it.

In America, the new ideas launched the American Revolution. Thomas Jefferson wrote the ideas down in the Declaration of Independence. People are "endowed by their Creator with certain unalienable Rights." He went on to say that in order to protect those rights "Governments are instituted among Men, deriving their just powers from the consent of the governed." People give government the right to rule. And if government fails to protect the rights of the people, "it is the Right of the People to alter or to abolish" that government and form a "new Government."

Today—because of the Declaration of Independence and the American Revolution—Americans have a representative government. We are not subjects of our government. We are citizens responsible for our government. We are people engaged in making our homes, our schools, our places of work, our communities, our states, and even the nation a better place for us all.

TELLING GOVERNMENT WHAT TO DO

So if the people—the citizens—are in charge of the government, we tell our government what to do. In a perfect world, we would just tell our representatives what we want, and government would do it. Leaders or elected representatives can't just do anything they want. They have a responsibility to the people. But nothing is ever that simple.

For one thing, citizens may not agree among themselves what they want. For another, government is made up of people too, and government officials have their own ideas about how things should work. So we don't all always agree with the decisions our leaders make. That doesn't necessarily mean they are bad decisions. Most times our leaders are honestly trying to do the right thing. But sometimes they do make bad decisions that the majority of the people they represent do not agree with. In those cases, how do "We the People" make our representatives accountable?

Elections are one way. If we don't like the way someone is representing us, we can go to the polls and vote to replace that representative with someone else.

Even so, it takes more than just one vote to make a change. We have to gather like-minded people together and work to increase the size of the group.

BUT GOVERNMENT MAKES THE LAW.

Governments make laws. That's what they do. And good citizens obey the laws. The problem is that sometimes government makes a law we don't agree with. What do we do then?

We know that we have to have laws. Laws and rules help us live together. But sometimes we look at a law and think it's not right or not fair. We want our laws to be good and right and fair—to be ethical. When we run across a law that isn't, we work to change the law.

Once in a while it's easy. You go to your representative and say, "That's not fair." Your representative says, "You're right. We will change it." But most of the time, it is a long and hard journey because we have to convince other people—citizens like us—that we should make a change. The tool we often use is protest. We demonstrate and persuade others to join our cause. And when there are enough citizens demanding a change, leaders and representatives will work to make the change. If they don't do what the people want, the people vote others into their offices who will do the right thing.

Now, here's the tricky part. We believe that good citizens—ethical citizens—obey the law. And there are lots of legal ways to protest. We can vote. We can write down our opinions and share them with others. We can speak respectfully at public gatherings. We can get a permit to hold a parade or demonstration. But American citizens don't always obey the law. There are times when we break the law to do what we think is right. What do we do with protesters who break laws? Protesters have to be willing to pay for the consequences of their actions. And sometimes it is a heavy price.

That's just what happened during the American Revolution. The Revolution got started because the colonists protested the way King George and the British Parliament treated them. They looked at the laws passed in England and decided they were not right. They were unethical, and the colonists were determined to change them. Things started out with public gatherings and demonstrations to express their point of view.

STAMP IT OUT.

Richard Henry Lee stood near the Westmoreland County, Virginia, Courthouse. It was September 24, 1765, and this was going to be a fun night. Everything was arranged.

Lee was an important man. He came from an old Virginia family. His great-grandfather came to Virginia in 1639. Richard Henry was part of a big family. He had five brothers and two sisters, and the family owned a lot of land. His father, uncles, and brothers were all involved in government.

Richard Henry Lee was picked by the governor of Virginia to be one of the Westmoreland County magistrates. A magistrate sat on the county court. The court decided simple cases like "Joe Smith owes me money" and "Linda Doe let her cow eat the grass in my yard." Local magistrates also looked out for the poor and orphans. They made sure the community roads and buildings were maintained, that kind of stuff. Mostly it was just boring everyday community business.

PRIVATE WEALTH
COMMON WEALTH

Richard Henry Lee had a lot of private wealth—money, power, and political position. And he used that private wealth to influence how the community thought about the Stamp Act. Is it right for wealthy and powerful people to influence the future of our common wealth this way?

But this day was special. The magistrates decided earlier in the morning to protest the Stamp Act by resigning. That meant there would be no county court meetings, no debts collected, no property sales recorded, no repairs to local roads, no one to look out for the poor and orphans—you get the picture. It was a big deal in Westmoreland County.

LAW / ETHICS

Would you give up your spot on, say, a sports team if the school or the coach wanted you to cheat or do something else you felt was unethical? Or would you just go with the flow?

But it wasn't enough for the magistrates just to resign in protest. Everyone in the county needed to know and understand. In eighteenth-century Virginia not everyone could read, so publishing their resignation letter in the newspaper might only reach a few people. So Richard Henry Lee was creating a pageant—a demonstration—for that night. Everyone in Westmoreland County would come and see why getting rid of the Stamp Act was so important.

What was the Stamp Act? It was a tax passed by the British Parliament, and it required colonists to use special stamped paper for all kinds of things, including ship's papers, legal documents, licenses, newspapers, publications, even decks of playing cards. But Parliament was in London, more than 3,500 miles away. How could they know what was best for Americans? Colonists decided that they couldn't. They decided that Parliament didn't care what was best for America and that the Stamp Tax was unfair.

UP IN FLAMES

"Mama wouldn't let me go see it last night," huffed Charlotte. "She treats me like a little girl." Charlotte was just past her twelfth birthday. "I heard it. And I could see the light from the fire. Did you see?"

"Oh my, yes, I saw it," said Hannah.

Hannah's father ran a small tavern near the courthouse. Charlotte's father farmed a few acres of tobacco not quite two miles from Westmoreland County Courthouse. The two girls were just about the same age and fast friends.

"I was there!" Hannah continued. "Papa let me come along with him and Thomas!"

"You have to tell me everything you saw," demanded Charlotte. "I want all the details."

"It was quite a site, that's for sure," said Hannah. "Papa said the whole thing was meant to tell us a story, to explain why the Stamp Act is bad. But I had to ask Thomas to explain some of it to me. It didn't all make sense." Thomas was Hannah's brother. He was sixteen and helped his father at the tavern. More importantly, Thomas was always listening to the men talk about politics. He really loved a good political argument.

"Tell me what happened!" Charlotte demanded.

Hannah set her sewing aside and looked steadily at Charlotte.

"It all happened right outside our tavern and across the way at the courthouse. Papa did not want to get too far away from the tavern, just in case the crowd got out of hand, so I stood there with Papa and Thomas right near our front stoop. It was a big crowd."

"How many people?" Charlotte wanted to know.

"It must have been near two hundred. I swear it was as big as any court day you ever saw. And all the magistrates were there."

"What about the ladies?" Charlotte always wanted to know what the ladies were wearing.

"I didn't see any of the real fancy ladies. None of the magistrates' wives with all their finery. Old Mrs. Campbell was there in the thick of it. Scolding folks and whacking them with her cane. And I saw Mrs. Whittman too. She was there with her husband and son. But there were not many women about the crowd. They were a rowdy bunch. Lots of young men. There were laboring men and women for sure. And a lot of slaves. Tag, rag, and bobtails—everyone all mixed up together."

UNITY
DIVERSITY

When the community gathers together, you realize we are not all alike. We are men and women, rich and poor, different races, in eighteenth-century Virginia enslaved and free. Still, with all that diversity, you can see the community come together to work, celebrate, and even protest.

"There were gentlemen there, weren't there?"

"Oh my, yes! A few of the magistrates and other gentlemen. Richard Henry Lee was there. He's a handsome figure. And he's the one who made the pageant."

Charlotte looked quizzical. *"He* made the pageant?"

"Aye," Hannah nodded. "The whole thing was his idea, Papa says. And Mr. Lee brought all his people and wagons and such to make everything work. It was a grand parade, for sure."

"Parade?"

"It started with two of Mr. Lee's slaves. They led the parade carrying long clubs, like they were soldiers guarding something. And they were dressed fine. Next came the whole mob of people. All the folks from the county all mixed up

together and cheering and yelling. Then came a horse and cart. In the cart were these two straw men, like scarecrows, except they had signs on them. The first wore a sign that said he was George Grenville. Thomas said that's the man over in Britain who started this whole Stamp Act business. The other one was called George Mercer. He's the man the king appointed to be the collector of stamps for Virginia. That straw man had one sign that said 'Money is my God' and another that said 'Slavery I love.'"

FREEDOM

EQUALITY

The freedom to speak our minds—protest—is one of our most important rights. And it is one freedom we all share equally.

"What in the world does that mean?" Charlotte questioned.

"Thomas says that a tax collector, like the stamp collector, makes a lot of money. Everyone is saying that this man named Mercer took the job as stamp collector so he could get rich. And Thomas says that taxing the colonies this way is not right. It's like the king and Parliament turning us all into slaves."

"Oh, I suppose," Charlotte replied. "Was that all?"

"Oh, no!" said Hannah. "There were some of Mr. Lee's slaves guarding the straw men. Thomas said they represented the sheriffs, jailers, and other officials in Virginia. You see, . . ."

"Yes, I do see!" exclaimed Charlotte. "By using his slaves in the parade, Mr. Lee was showing us that all of Virginia government was enslaved by the Stamp Act."

"Indeed! And then right after the cart came Mr. Richard Henry Lee. He is such a gentleman. He walked so proud. His head up high. He wore a sword and carried a cane.

It looked like his waistcoat just shimmered in the light of the torches. After they paraded a while with all the yelling and cheering, Mr. Lee stopped everyone. They pulled up under the big tree over by the old Carroll place, that little shack where nobody lives anymore. They put ropes around the necks of those straw men like they were going to hang them. Then Mr. Lee gave the dying speech of Mr. George Mercer."

"Dying speech?" Charlotte questioned. "But George Mercer weren't there. He's not going to die, is he? I mean, they didn't go kill him, did they?"

"No! My word! Nothing like that. It's make-believe. But they want to send a message to George Mercer. They don't like him agreeing to be the stamp collector." Hannah was shaking her head to make sure Charlotte was getting the point.

"And what a fine voice Mr. Lee has," Hannah continued. "Just as clear and strong as a bell it is. He said how Mr. Mercer was sorry for what he'd done and how he was sorry he had hurt Virginia. Then he said some foreign words. Thomas said it was Latin, but he didn't know what it meant." Hannah paused to catch her breath for a bit.

"So that was it?" Charlotte asked.

"My, no!" Hannah smiled. "Then they burned the straw men right up. It musta been really dry straw 'cause it went up in a big bright flame. But it wasn't enough for some of the crowd. They wanted more, so they set fire to the old Carroll place, and it went up in flames too!"

"No wonder I could see the fires from my house! It musta been a sight."

"It was . . . it was," Hannah nodded. "By then the crowd was getting a bit unruly, and Papa made me go back in the house, but you could hear them for hours singing and laughing and drinking and making a fuss. They say it was all such a big lot of fun they might come back and do it again tonight all over again!"

"Oh, my word," mumbled Charlotte, and she started plotting how she could slip away from her mother this night. No way was she going to miss the fun tonight.

This was a peaceful protest for the most part—a demonstration to help get people behind the cause for American liberty. But in the end Americans would break the law and take up arms against their government—the king and Parliament of Great Britain. Treason is a very serious crime. And there were consequences. Eight long years of warfare. Many died. Many lost their families, their property. The Revolutionary generation gave up a lot for what they believed in.

PROTESTING THE PROTESTERS

History—looking back at what happened—often helps us see the good changes that protest can bring. Look at the American Revolution for example. There were Loyalists who thought that protesting against the British government was dumb. But, today, who would say that the American Revolution was a bad thing?

At the time of the protest, there's always somebody on the other side, people who think that things are just fine like they are or that the problem should be solved a different way. So, often you find that the protesters are being protested by protesters. After all, protesting is part of the conversation that we—the citizens—have with each other.

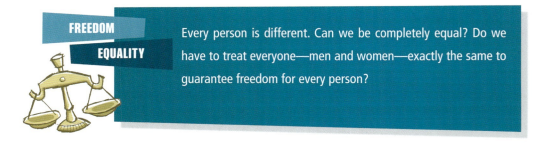

FREEDOM

EQUALITY

Every person is different. Can we be completely equal? Do we have to treat everyone—men and women—exactly the same to guarantee freedom for every person?

"ALL MEN AND WOMEN ARE CREATED EQUAL."

How long does it take for a protest to work? The Revolution started when colonists protested the Stamp Act in 1765 and ended with the Treaty of Paris in 1783—almost twenty years. The first abolitionist society in America was formed in 1775, but it took ninety years (until 1865) before the Thirteenth Amendment ended slavery in the United States. The women's rights movement is another long protest movement.

In 1848, the first women's rights convention was held in Seneca Falls, New York. The delegates who attended the Seneca Falls Convention created a document called the Declaration of Sentiments. Delegates used the Declaration of Independence as a model and called for women to have political, social, and economic equality with men. The Declaration of Sentiments stated, "All men and women are created equal."

But saying it did not make it so. Women protested to have their equality and their right to vote recognized. And they protested. And they protested. And they protested some more. It wasn't until 1920 that the Nineteenth Amendment to the Constitution recognized women's right to vote. That's seventy-two years after the Seneca Falls convention. And many people say that men and women today are still not treated equally, that there is still more to do. Sometimes it takes a long time for things to change.

There were people who disagreed with women's suffrage (the right to vote). All along the way—for all seventy-two years—there were protesters yelling that the women's rights protest was wrong. And some of those voices were downright nasty.

POSTAGE POSTCARD PROTEST

Protesters against women's suffrage accused women's rights supporters (called *suffragettes*) of destroying the values of American society. And if women destroyed American values, they would destroy America. The anti–women's rights protesters used everything they could think of to make their point.

In the late nineteenth and early twentieth centuries, cards and postcards were new and trendy. One of the ways the antisuffrage protesters spread their message was by sending political cartoon postcards to friends and acquaintances. Look at some of the stuff they were sending.

In America, it's always a good thing to connect to the Founders—the Revolutionary generation that founded the country. And the greatest Founder of them all was George Washington, the father of our country.

If George likes it, it's good. If he hates it, it's bad. Pretty simple, right? Except that George isn't really around to say what he thinks. Instead, we put words into his mouth. Like in the cartoon.

Did George think that "Votes for Women" was a bad thing? Or was that what the person who drew the cartoon was thinking?

And why, you ask, should anyone be against "Votes for Women"? Well, according to the cartoon below, if women got the vote, then they would wear pants, smoke tobacco, listen to music, and leave fathers at home alone to watch the kids. No stay-at-home dads for the antisuffrage generation.

Men at the time thought about themselves as out on the town enjoying popular culture while women stayed home. Can you imagine telling a woman today that she can't wear pants or listen to music?

Some people associate protesters with breaking the law. It happens. Sometimes protesters do some inappropriate things, such as blocking streets or entrances to buildings. This cartoon suggested that suffragettes attacked the police. The artist wanted people to believe that suffragettes were violent and that, if you supported votes for women, you were supporting lawbreakers.

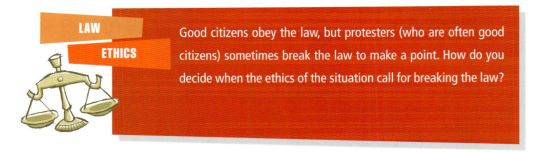

LAW
ETHICS

Good citizens obey the law, but protesters (who are often good citizens) sometimes break the law to make a point. How do you decide when the ethics of the situation call for breaking the law?

As the movement gained strength, suffragettes were often arrested for protesting. In 1872 Susan B. Anthony and several other women were arrested when they tried to vote. And many activists, like Lucy Burns and Alice Paul, were arrested for protesting. There are consequences when you break the law, and ethical people accept those consequences. They protest for their cause even if it means going to jail.

Sometimes the reaction against the protesters was severe. In March 1913 an antisuffragette mob forced a women's rights parade in Washington, D.C., to stop. Dozens of women marchers were injured when the police were unable to protect them. In 1917 women staged an illegal protest outside the White House. They were arrested, but when the protesters were taken to the Occoquan Workhouse in Northern Virginia, they were attacked and harassed by their jailers.

Americans were shocked when they learned how the women had been mistreated at the Occoquan Workhouse. The stories caused people to pay attention. Courts ruled that the protesters had been arrested illegally. President Woodrow Wilson declared his support for women's suffrage. In 1919 Congress passed an amendment to the Constitution finally recognizing women's right to vote. The Nineteenth Amendment was ratified by the states the following year.

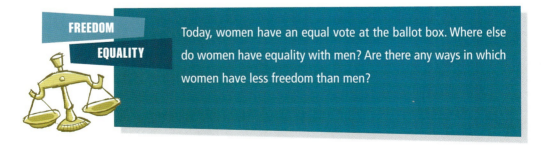

FREEDOM

EQUALITY

Today, women have an equal vote at the ballot box. Where else do women have equality with men? Are there any ways in which women have less freedom than men?

There was a real sense of optimism in 1920. You can see it in this *New York Times* political cartoon. People hoped that suffrage—the right to vote—would provide women opportunities that were not available before. Those opportunities were listed on the rungs of the ladder that would lift the young woman in the cartoon skyward. Now women could expect equal pay, "positions of trust," and "high executive offices."

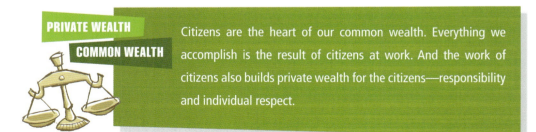

PRIVATE WEALTH
COMMON WEALTH

Citizens are the heart of our common wealth. Everything we accomplish is the result of citizens at work. And the work of citizens also builds private wealth for the citizens—responsibility and individual respect.

But recognizing a woman's right to vote did not end the debate. It continues today. In 1923 suffragettes argued that the right to vote was not enough. They proposed an equal rights amendment to the Constitution: "Equality of rights under the law shall not be denied or abridged . . . on account of sex." Thirty-eight states (three-fourths of the states) have to ratify the amendment for it to become part of the Constitution. The Equal Rights Amendment has never been ratified by enough states to become law.

The ethical issue is still there, and we continue to discuss it. Do women have equal opportunities in the workplace? Are women and men treated equally before the law? Should women be allowed to work in every job? Those and other questions are still before us. And protesters on both sides march and demonstrate, publish, and meet to declare their opinions.

RIDING THE RAILS

In 1890 the quickest way to get anywhere—to the next town, across the state, or across the country—was by train. Train tracks crisscrossed the nation. Train stations were one of the places where Americans of every race gathered. And that was a problem.

Remember, the 1890s were the era of Jim Crow laws—laws that limited the rights of African Americans. In 1890 the legislature of Louisiana passed one of those laws. The Separate Car Act said that blacks and whites had to travel in separate railroad cars.

Some African American businessmen in Louisiana took steps to protest the law. They convinced a young African American by the name of Homer Plessy to travel in a whites-only train car. In 1892 Plessy went to the train station in New Orleans and bought a first-class ticket to ride on the East Louisiana Railroad. He went onto the whites-only first-class car and took a seat. When they told him to move to the "colored" car, Plessy said, "No!" He was arrested and went on trial. A judge named John Howard Ferguson ruled it was OK for Louisiana to make railroad companies segregate their customers. Ferguson ordered Plessy to pay a fine. Plessy appealed his case to higher courts. The case became known as *Plessy v. Ferguson.*

Homer Plessy's court case went all the way to the Supreme Court of the United States. Mr. Plessy's lawyers argued that his arrest violated the Fourteenth Amendment to the Constitution, which said, "No State shall make or enforce any law which shall abridge the privileges or immunities of citizens of the United States." Plessy was, after all, a citizen of the United States.

Unfortunately, the Supreme Court did not agree. The court said it was OK for states to separate the races, especially since the train cars—white and black—were equal.

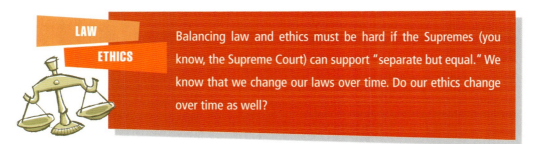

LAW / ETHICS

Balancing law and ethics must be hard if the Supremes (you know, the Supreme Court) can support "separate but equal." We know that we change our laws over time. Do our ethics change over time as well?

The *Plessy v. Ferguson* Supreme Court case launched a whole series of new Jim Crow laws because the Supremes declared that separate but equal facilities were A-OK. And so the races were separated—separate public restrooms, water fountains, schools, transportation, seating areas, restaurants, and on and on it went.

Of course the facilities were separate, but they were not equal. African Americans got the poorest quality of everything. It was demeaning—a put-down on a national scale.

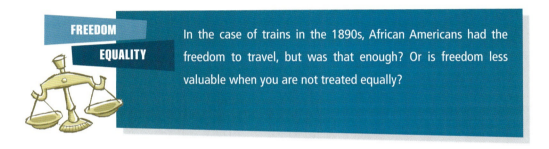

FREEDOM
EQUALITY

In the case of trains in the 1890s, African Americans had the freedom to travel, but was that enough? Or is freedom less valuable when you are not treated equally?

The civil rights movement gained steam in the 1950s and 1960s, and the story moved to buses. African Americans challenged Jim Crow laws, and they were making progress. In 1946 they won a victory in a case called *Irene Morgan v. Commonwealth of Virginia*.

Miss Morgan pulled a kind of Homer Plessy move. She got on a bus in Maryland, and when the bus crossed over into Virginia, she was told she had to move to segregated seating. She said no and was arrested. But this time the Supreme Court came down in her favor. The trouble was that, even though she won the court case, no one in the federal government enforced the law. All over the South, transportation companies, states, and local communities made African Americans sit in separate sections from whites.

WHO SAYS WE DO IT THAT WAY?

Protesters challenge not only laws but also other kinds of rules. Sometimes protesters challenge the idea that "it's just the way we do things."

In 1961 the laws of the federal government were on the side of African Americans. Federal law regulated transportation between states. It's called *interstate commerce,* and the Constitution gives the federal government authority to regulate interstate commerce. Supreme Court cases made it illegal for interstate transportation companies and the states to segregate seating. And that wasn't just on the buses. That also included bus terminals that served interstate traffic. But there were local laws and state laws that contradicted the federal laws. And there was custom—"just the way we do things." At that point, local and state laws and custom were winning. Across the South, African Americans still faced discrimination.

A group calling themselves Freedom Riders planned a protest. Thirteen people—seven African Americans and six whites—participated in a plan organized by a group called the Congress for Racial Equality (CORE). It was a simple plan. Leave Washington, D.C., on May 4, 1961, and ride interstate buses all the way to New Orleans. The plan was to arrive in New Orleans on May 17, where a civil rights rally was planned. These protesters knew that riding together broke local and state laws, but they hoped their protest would change the rules for "the way we do things here."

CHAPTER 2: PROTESTING

FREEDOM RIDERS TRAIL 1961

1. Washington, DC, May 1–3: Thirteen volunteers assemble for training in nonviolent protest. They are ready to be arrested and pledge that they will not resist or become violent, no matter what happens to them.

2. Washington, DC, May 4: The Riders board buses. The plan for each bus: One African American will ride in the front section reserved for "whites only." A white Freedom Rider and a black Freedom Rider will sit together (against the rules too). One Freedom Rider will obey all the rules so that if something happens (like someone gets arrested), that Rider can report in and call for help. Everyone anxiously waits to see what will happen when they cross into Virginia.

3. Fredericksburg, VA, May 4: Riders ignore the "white only" and "colored only" signs, and there are no reactions from officials.

4. Richmond, VA, May 4–5: The buses arrive in Richmond, and the group spends the night at Virginia Union University. They depart the following morning. There are no incidents.

5. Petersburg, VA, May 5–6: There are no incidents in Petersburg either. The Riders attend a rally at the Bethany Baptist Church that evening and depart the next morning.

6. Farmville, VA, May 6: At this rest stop, the Riders discover that the signs for separate "white" and "colored" facilities have been painted over. They are surprised, and they are not harassed.

7. Lynchburg, VA, May 6–7: Again, the Riders find no problems and spend the night in the homes of local church members.

8. Danville, VA, May 7: At this rest stop, they meet their first resistance when a white Rider sits at the "colored" lunch counter. The African American waiter tells him that his boss threatened to fire him if he serves a Freedom Rider.

9. Greensboro, NC, May 7: After arriving, the Riders meet with activists at Shiloh Baptist Church.

10. Salisbury, NC, May 8: At this rest stop, the Riders find segregation signs, but no one enforces them.

11. Charlotte, NC, May 8: Joseph Perkins, a black man, is arrested because he sits at a whites-only shoeshine stand. He refuses to pay the fifty dollars for bail and spends two nights in jail.

12. Rock Hill, SC, May 8: John Lewis, a black man, is assaulted when he tries to enter the bus terminal's whites-only waiting room. Fellow Rider Al Bigelow, who is white, is also assaulted. (In 1987 John Lewis was elected U.S. representative for Georgia's Fifth Congressional District.)

13. Winnsboro, SC, May 9: Hank Thomas, a black man, and the white James Peck sit together to order lunch and are arrested for attempting to integrate the bus station lunch counter.

14. Sumter, SC, May 10–11: The Freedom Riders take two days to rest and recuperate.

15. Sumter, SC, May 12: The Riders depart.

PRIVATE WEALTH
COMMON WEALTH

Your life and well-being are your most treasured private wealth. Are you prepared to give them up to make the whole community—our common wealth—better? The Freedom Riders were.

FREEDOM RIDERS TRAIL 1961

16 Augusta, GA, May 12: No problems at the Augusta bus terminal. They spend the night and depart the following morning.

17 Atlanta, GA, May 13: After a stop in Athens, Georgia, the Freedom Riders arrive in Atlanta with no problems. They meet with Dr. Martin Luther King Jr. and learn that there is a plot to disrupt the ride in Alabama.

18 South of Anniston, AL, May 14: The first bus is flagged down before reaching town. The bus driver is warned that a mob is waiting for them in Anniston.

19. Anniston, AL, May 14: A mob blocks the first bus, screams threats, breaks windows, slashes tires, and threatens the Riders. Police arrive, but they are in league with the mob. Police escort the damaged bus to the edge of town.

20. The second bus arrives in Anniston, but, before it can depart, Klansmen enter the bus and demand that the Riders sit in segregated seats. When the Riders (both black and white) refuse, they are beaten and dragged to the rear of the bus. The police refuse to interfere.

21. Bynum, AL, May 14: The first bus is forced off the road. Highway patrolmen arrive but stand aside and watch. For twenty minutes, the Ku Klux Klan (KKK) attacks the bus. They set fire to the bus and bar the doors hoping to kill the Freedom Riders in the inferno. Fortunately the Riders escape.

22. Birmingham, AL, May 14: At the terminal, members of the KKK are awaiting the arrival of the second bus. They arrange with police to have fifteen minutes and use the time to attack the Freedom Riders and bystanders with pipes, chains, and clubs.

23. May 15: Television, radio, and newspaper stories all over the country tell of the attacks on the Freedom Riders. White supremacists blame the Freedom Riders. But many Americans are outraged. A lot of Americans had come to accept segregation as a way of life—just how things were. But the violence against the Freedom Riders caused people to ask themselves, "Is this right?"

24. Birmingham, AL, May 15: Alabama governor John Patterson refuses to guarantee safe passage for the Freedom Riders. Bus drivers—afraid for their lives—refuse to drive. The Freedom Riders decide that they must abandon the bus trip. They fly to New Orleans.

UNITY

DIVERSITY

So, you go along thinking, "This is just how everybody does it." Then suddenly someone sees it differently. Does it make you question whether the "how everybody does it" is right? Or do you stick with the group?

The KKK, white supremacists, and segregationists thought they had won, but on May 17 more Freedom Riders arrived in Birmingham. They were college students from Nashville, Tennessee, inspired by what the original thirteen had accomplished. When they arrived in Birmingham, they were arrested. But the protest didn't stop. More protesters arrived all through the summer. Hundreds participated. Hundreds were arrested. But they just kept coming.

By the end of May, other organizations had joined CORE, which had organized the original protest, including the Student Nonviolent Coordinating Committee (SNCC) and the Southern Christian Leadership Conference (SCLC). They broke the law. They broke the rules. They challenged "the way we do things here." They also suffered some pretty harsh consequences—jail time, violence, and more. And they inspired the whole nation because they were doing what was right—what was ethical.

WHAT ARE *YOU* GOING TO PROTEST?

Protest is what Americans do. When we see something we don't think is right, we protest. It isn't always a big parade with signs and slogans. Citizens protest in a lot of different ways.

We might look at a business and decide, for example, that the owners don't treat their employees fairly. Citizens might protest that business by boycotting—just refusing to do any business with that company. If enough citizens boycott, the business has to change or close down.

Maybe we decide that our local government isn't doing what's best for our school. Students, parents, and teachers might protest. They might show up at a school board meeting to march outside the building, hold up signs during the meeting, or speak in front of the school board. When they do, they are citizens exercising their right to protest.

Maybe it isn't a law or an organization. Maybe it's just the way we do things. And everyone has done it that way so long most people don't even think about whether it's fair or right. But if we see it's unjust—unethical—don't we have a responsibility as citizens to speak up?

After all, that's how we create our laws. Citizens see a problem that needs to be solved. We gather together in groups to discuss and debate the problem. We can demonstrate and protest to help convince others that our ideas about how to solve the problem are the best ideas. Sometimes it takes a long time to work through our solutions, but eventually our representatives create a law to help solve the problem. Once we have created a law, we expect that good citizens will follow the law, that they will act responsibly and ethically according to the law.

It's a constant process. We have to work at it all the time. We need laws and rules to protect us. They help us get things done in our communities. They help us live together. But, sometimes, citizens scratch their heads. Maybe the law or rule used to work OK, but maybe things have changed and it just doesn't work anymore. Maybe it's just unfair. Maybe it's just not right. When that happens, it's up to citizens to get the law or rule changed—to make it better. And protesting is one very important tool. With protest, courageous citizens can get the job done.

But it's not an easy decision. Sometimes there are consequences. Protesters are sometimes harassed. Sometimes they're arrested. Sometimes they're hurt. Being a citizen is hard work.

ARE YOU UP TO IT?

ARE YOU WILLING TO MAKE A DIFFERENCE?

ARE YOU WILLING TO STAND FOR BOTH LAW AND ETHICS?

ALL THE NOISE

You hear it all the time. "Go to school, get good grades, and work hard so you can get a good job when you grow up." Are you tired of hearing it yet? Just wait. You have high school and then college or a training school of some kind. Everyone seems hyperfocused on the "be successful" thing. Parents and family members tell you what they expect. Scout leaders, sports coaches, religious leaders, and others tell you what they expect. Teachers, principals, and school counselors tell you what they expect. It seems like everyone has a plan for your life, and they all have something to say about your education.

It's important. There's no doubt about that, but the pressure can be pretty intense. Sometimes you just wish that you could shut it all out and just listen to yourself—decide what it is that you want. This is, after all, a time in your life when lightbulbs start to go off. It starts to dawn on you that you've got a great future ahead. You can be whatever you want to be. Right now all those activities at home, at school, and in the community are creating the real you. You are learning skills, gaining knowledge, and shaping the experiences that will help you become a good citizen. And that responsibility—becoming a good citizen—is the journey of a lifetime.

MAKE SOME WEALTH

There are two things going on at the same time. First, by becoming educated and learning to be successful, you are creating private wealth. That's the kind of wealth that makes *you* richer. Sometimes the wealth is money. Education may help you get a good job in the future. But money isn't the only wealth you create. Friendships and relationships with other people make you richer. We're all human, and sharing our lives with other people is important to us. Knowledge is an important kind of wealth. The ability to accomplish things, work out problems, lead others, and inspire people is important. These abilities along with other skills are valuable. Sometimes the wealth you create is spiritual. That kind of inner peace can enrich your life. There are hundreds of ways you can create wealth for and within yourself.

But there's something else going on in your life right now. You're creating another kind of wealth by learning how to be a successful citizen. Americans have always believed that an educated citizen is a better citizen—a responsible citizen. We've already seen that citizenship is hard and difficult work. It takes dedication. Citizens have to think through the consequences of their actions. Citizenship means that we can and will engage in the Great Debate, that we will work with each other to create solutions for the problems and issues that face our community, our state, our nation, and our world. Good citizens—together—build our common wealth.

Education in our Republic—your education—develops both private wealth and common wealth.

Not everyone begins this education journey in the same place and with the same resources. Some of us are disadvantaged. We don't read quite so well. Or we have trouble with math. Some people are great athletes. Some are not. Some catch onto new ideas quickly. Some of us are a bit slower on the uptake. But Americans believe that every individual can be successful. Every individual can make a contribution.

We believe in setting our own goals, taking advantage of the opportunities presented to us, and creating our own success.

DREAMING LIKE AN AMERICAN

Lots of people talk about the American dream. Ever wonder what that means? For most Americans it means that we can shape our own futures. We can create lives for ourselves. We can be individuals. We can be free. Americans don't expect that we will be handed what we dream. We just want the opportunity to create our dreams for ourselves. To be successful.

Thomas Jefferson's father, Peter Jefferson, did not have much formal education. He was a surveyor (someone who measures land) and cartographer (someone who draws maps). The map of Virginia that he and his partner Joshua Fry drew and published in 1751 was the best, most accurate map available. They were the first to get the Allegheny Mountains right. They were the first to chart the Great Wagon Road that ran from Philadelphia through the Shenandoah Valley, Roanoke Valley, and New River Valley to the Yadkin River in North Carolina. No big deal today. We just pull out our cell phones, call up the satellite image, and bang! In an instant we know where we are and just what it all looks like. But Peter, Joshua, and other surveyors had to go out on foot to measure and draw this map, yard by yard. A big job, right?

Even though Peter Jefferson did not have much formal education, he loved reading. He loved books. Perhaps that's why his son Tom developed such a thirst for education. Peter Jefferson was able to use his position as a surveyor to buy land. He became wealthy enough that he could send Tom to school. And in those days you had to have money to get an education. There weren't any public schools, where learning was free. Peter Jefferson first paid for his son to attend a local school run by a Presbyterian minister. But then Thomas Jefferson's father died, at only forty-nine years old. Tom was only fourteen.

Losing his father could have changed everything, but Tom kept going to school. He went to the Reverend James Maury's school for two years. Next it was on to the College of William and Mary in Williamsburg, Virginia, and finally he studied law with George Wythe in Williamsburg.

Tom was lucky. He was able to pay for his education. Most people could not pay. A boy might stay home and learn farming from his father. Or a daughter might stay home and learn housewifery (how to run a home) from her mother. And some kids might get apprenticeships.

WHAT'S THE MYSTERY?

An apprenticeship was a contract between a kid of say twelve or thirteen and a master tradesman or woman. They called that kind of contract an *indenture*. The tradesman or woman promised to teach the kid a useful trade, like shoemaking or blacksmithing or millinery, and the apprentice agreed to work for the trades person without pay until he or she was twenty-one years old. Ready to sign up? Pages 84–85 show what an apprenticeship contract looked like.

apprenticeship contract

Francis Moss is the young man who agrees to be the apprentice.

Approbation means "with approval."

So, at the age of twelve or thirteen, Francis agrees to all this stuff, and he signs a legal document! Would your parent or guardian let you do that?

John Draper is a blacksmith. He makes and repairs all kinds of iron and steel objects. A pretty useful trade, wouldn't you say?

Six whole years Francis has to work!

So it's part of the legal contract that Francis has to obey his teacher. Bet your teacher would like that.

Francis even has to promise that he is going to take care of his teacher's tools and supplies and property—do no damage!

Nope! No gambling! And certainly don't make a bet with the teacher's property!

This Indenture Witnesseth That Francis Moss of the County of York by approbation of the Court of the County aforesaid and his own Consent hath put himself, and by these presents doth voluntarily and of his own free will and accord put himself apprentice to John Draper of the City of Williamsburg to learn his Art Trade and Mystery and after the Manner of an Apprentice to serve the said John Draper from the Day of the Date hereof for and During and unto the full end and Term of Six Years during all which Term the said Apprentice his said Master faithfully shall serve his Secrets keep his Lawfull Commands at all Times readily Obey: He shall do no Damage to his said Master, nor see it be done by others without giving Notice thereof to his said Master. He shall not waste his said Masters Goods nor lend them unlawfully to any. He shall not . . . contract Matrimony within the said Term. At Cards Dice or any other unlawfull Game he shall not play whereby his said Master may have Damage With his own Goods nor the Goods of others without License from his Master he shall not buy nor sell. He shall not absent himself

Day or Night from his said Masters Service without his Leave nor haunt Alehouses Taverns or playhouses but in all Things, behave himself as a faithful apprentice ought to do during the said Term. And the said Master shall use the utmost of his Endeavours to teach or Cause to be taught or instructed the said Apprentice in the Trade or Mystery of a Blacksmith and procure or provide for him sufficient Meat Drink Cloathes Washing and Lodging fitting for an apprentice during the said Term of Six Years also teach him to read and write with freedom Dues. And for the true performance of all and singular the Covenants and Agreements aforesaid the parties bind themselves each unto the other firmly by these presents. In Witness whereof the said Parties have interchangeably set their Hands and Seals hereunto Dated the Twentieth day of May in the Eleventh Year of the Reign of our Sovereign Lord George the Third King of Great Britain &c. Anno Domini One Thousand Seven hundred and seventy one.

John Draper

Sealed and Delivered
In the Presence of

Francis Moss

- Can you imagine having your teacher around all the time—day and night? Always teaching? Always correcting everything you do?

- No fun or entertainment. Can't go to the tavern or playhouse, can't go to a theater. Today, they'd probably ban candy, sodas, video games, and social media too!

- Finally, the contract tells us what the teacher has to do!

- Here's the "mystery" part. At the end of six years, Francis will have learned everything he needs to know—all the "Trade or Mystery"—to become a successful blacksmith.

- The teacher agrees to feed Francis, provide his clothing, do his laundry, and give him a place to live.

- You can't run a successful blacksmithing business unless you can read and write, so the teacher agrees to make sure Francis learns that as well.

- Freedom dues are like a graduation present. At the end of the apprenticeship, the teacher will give Francis a set of tools and a suit of clothes so he can go out and start working for himself.

What do you think? Are you ready to move in with your teacher and work night and day for the next six or seven years? No movies, no television, no video games, no social media. Just work. I wonder if your teacher's a good cook?

Today we think it's kind of a crazy way to go to school, but two hundred years ago this was a great opportunity for young Francis Moss. It would have given him a way to support himself and a family. He would have learned a trade that would have made him an important part of his community. It would have given him the opportunity to create private wealth and also make a contribution to the common wealth.

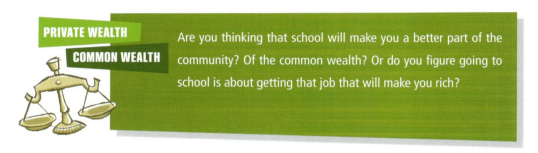

PRIVATE WEALTH
COMMON WEALTH

Are you thinking that school will make you a better part of the community? Of the common wealth? Or do you figure going to school is about getting that job that will make you rich?

We always think about education as creating private wealth. You hear it all the time. "To get a good job, you need to get a good education." And that certainly was the emphasis in the eighteenth century. Get a good job to support yourself and your family. But when the United States became an independent country, education became more important to the common wealth. Education wasn't just about private wealth. Education also helped build a stronger nation.

MAYBE IT'S NOT JUST ABOUT ME?

Some of that first bunch of Americans (we call them the Founders) started thinking that education was more than just getting a job. Not everyone was thinking about it the same way, though. It started a debate. One group of the new nation's leaders figured that the common people (people like you and me) should just leave the important stuff (like running the country) to well-educated leaders (like them). That's right. Just don't worry your little head. Go off and be a good worker, and let the smart people rule the country. Kind of snooty, huh?

Fortunately, there were some other leaders (like Thomas Jefferson) who said, "No way!" Tom figured the more the merrier. His idea was that the common people, people like you and me, should all participate in government. He believed that more democracy was better. In other words, in America everyday ordinary people should play a big role in running their government. The United States is, after all, a government of "We the People." Tom was pretty insistent about this. In fact, Tom had some great sayings about education that you still hear people repeat today.

THOMAS JEFFERSON

1778: "Those entrusted with power have, in time ... perverted it into tyranny; and it is believed that the most effectual means of preventing this would be, to illuminate, as far as practicable, the minds of the people at large." Translation: Citizens—people like you—need an education so they can keep powerful leaders in line.

1786: "Preach, my dear Sir, a crusade against ignorance; establish and improve the law for educating the common people." Translation: Make sure "We the People" are not stupid!

1816: "If a nation expects to be ignorant and free, in a state of civilisation, it expects what never was and never will be." Translation: You can't have a strong nation if the citizens are dumb.

FREEDOM
EQUALITY

Does education make us more free? Does education make us more equal?

1785: "What are the objects of an useful American education? Classical knowledge, modern languages and chiefly French, Spanish, and Italian; Mathematics; Natural philosophy; Natural History; Civil History; Ethics." Translation: Good citizens need a well-rounded education, including history!

1786: "I think by far the most important bill in our whole code is that for the diffusion of knowledge among the people. No other sure foundation can be devised for the preservation of freedom, and happiness." Translation: Educated citizens will protect freedom and happiness for all Americans.

LAW
ETHICS

Schools are so important that we make laws to regulate schools. Laws say when kids go to school, what they study, and who can teach. But how do we know that we're teaching the right things in our schools? Are you learning about ethics in school?

1820: "I know no safe depository of the ultimate powers of the society, but the people themselves: and if we think them not enlightened enough to exercise their controul with a wholsome discretion, the remedy is, not to take it from them, but to inform their discretion by education." Translation: Educate the people to make sure they can govern themselves responsibly.

CAN'T BE IGNORANT AND FREE

Thomas Jefferson's idea about the importance of education caught on. It was seen in the number of people who started reading newspapers, the number of books printed, the community organizations that gathered to talk about issues, and the public schools started in some states. Education was one of the ways that nineteenth-century Americans prepared for citizenship. And so it's no wonder that, after the Civil War, newly freed African Americans were hungry for education. For them, education was the way to defeat the old world (where they were enslaved) and create a new world (where African Americans were citizens of the United States).

You see, many slaveholders in the years before the Civil War believed that it was dangerous to educate the people they had enslaved. Education is powerful. Being able to read makes important information available. Writing makes it possible to communicate with others. White masters and mistresses worried that slaves would use those skills to communicate with each other and rebel against slavery, so in many places it was against the law to educate an enslaved person.

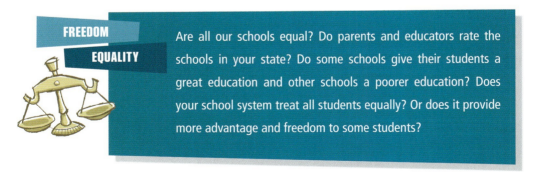

FREEDOM
EQUALITY

Are all our schools equal? Do parents and educators rate the schools in your state? Do some schools give their students a great education and other schools a poorer education? Does your school system treat all students equally? Or does it provide more advantage and freedom to some students?

During the Civil War, some African Americans escaped from slavery and joined the Union army. They were ready to fight for their freedom. But freedom was not just about fighting. It was also about becoming a citizen, and that required education. In 1864, E. S. Wheeler was a Union army chaplain serving with African American troops in Louisiana. He was impressed by these men who were former slaves and their thirst for education and said so in a letter to his superior officer.

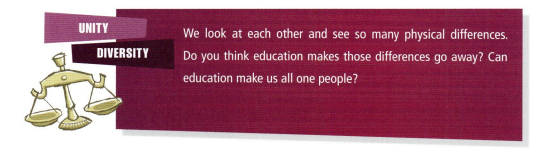

UNITY / DIVERSITY

We look at each other and see so many physical differences. Do you think education makes those differences go away? Can education make us all one people?

I am sure that I never witnessed greater eagerness for study. . . . A majority of the men seem to regard their books as an indispensable portion of their equipments, and the cartridge box [their ammunition] and spelling book are attached to the same belt. There are nearly five hundred men . . . who have learned to read quite well, and also quite a large number who are able to write. A short time ago scarcely one of these men knew a letter of the alphabet. . . . Instruction . . . has also been given in the Geography of the Country, especially as regards the States, their Capitals, rivers,

> population &c. The accomplishment of so much, under the circumstances, is an additional proof of the intellectual capacity of the race.

Can you imagine being an adult unable to read and write? Would you be embarrassed? Would you be willing to swallow your pride and start from the beginning? It would take a lot of courage to do it. But these soldiers understood that education was the pathway to a future for themselves and their families. Serving in the military was a way for these men to contribute to a new future for all Americans—a future without slavery. They were working to make a contribution to the common wealth of the country because educated citizens are better citizens. They understood that getting an education was a responsibility of good citizens.

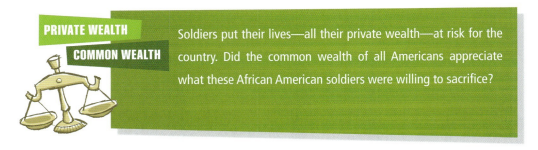

PRIVATE WEALTH
COMMON WEALTH

Soldiers put their lives—all their private wealth—at risk for the country. Did the common wealth of all Americans appreciate what these African American soldiers were willing to sacrifice?

As the Civil War was ending, the federal government set up the Freedmen's Bureau to help former slaves. Setting up schools was one very important job. They set up schools for children to attend in the day. Adults attended a night school after work. There were also industrial schools to teach work skills and Sunday schools for teaching religion.

LAW ETHICS

Congress passed a law to create the Freedmen's Bureau. The unethical slave laws were repealed. But could anything wipe out the memories of and damage done by American slavery?

> The pupils beg that the work may not be intermitted [stopped] for the necessary summer vacation; that, ordinarily, suspension from the privileges of the school is the severest punishment which the teacher needs to inflict; and that out of their poverty the colored people have made so large contributions for the purchase of land, the erection of buildings, and the support of teachers. More than half the schools in the South are sustained in part by the freedmen.

How about you? Do you think it's a privilege to go to school? Would you beg to stay in school, even through your summer vacation? To many, school is just something you have to do. But for these former enslaved men, women, and children, education was life changing. And it didn't stop with neighborhood schools. African Americans built colleges and universities too—Spelman College, Howard University, Hampton University, Morehouse College, Tuskegee University, Fisk University, and more. Education was the future.

EDUCATION CAN CHANGE YOU.

For African Americans after the Civil War, education was an opportunity to change. But education can also change us in ways that we don't want, that we don't like.

Think about all the immigrants who come to America. Our schools—our education system—help them become Americans. They integrate into our American society, into the way Americans think and do things. When that happens, they also can lose touch with the culture of their parents and the ways they lived and believed in their old country.

Native Americans were not immigrants, but, in the late nineteenth and early twentieth centuries, white Americans wanted Native people to give up their old ways. White Americans wanted to do away with Native American cultures. Schools were set up. Native American children were taken from their families and put in boarding schools, far from home, where they learned to be "modern" Americans.

I WILL NOT SUBMIT!

Zitkala-Sa traveled east with a group of children from her tribe, the Yankton. The group included her friends Judéwin and Thowin. At first Zitkala-Sa was excited to be going to visit a place she called "the land of apples." But the train ride frightened her. Everything was strange. The white people on the train stared and pointed at her. Even though she could not understand English, she knew that they were making fun of her. And it hurt. Years later Zitkala-Sa remembered her school days.

The first day in the land of apples was a bitter-cold one; for the snow still covered the ground, and the trees were bare. A large bell rang for breakfast. . . . And though my spirit tore itself in struggling for its lost freedom, all was useless.

. . . We were placed in a line of girls who were marching into the dining room. These were Indian girls, in stiff shoes and closely clinging dresses. . . . While we marched in, the boys entered at an opposite door. I watched for the three young braves who came in our party. I spied them in the rear ranks, looking as uncomfortable as I felt.

A small bell was tapped, and each of the pupils drew a chair from under the table. Supposing this act meant they were to be seated, I pulled out mine and at once slipped into it from one side. But when I turned my head, I saw that I was the only one seated, and all the rest at our table remained standing. Just as I began to rise, looking shyly around to see how chairs were to be used, a second bell was sounded. All were seated at last, and I had to crawl back into my chair again. I heard a man's voice at one end of the hall, and I looked around to see him. But all the others hung their heads over their plates. As I glanced at the long chain of tables, I caught the eyes of a paleface woman upon me. Immediately I dropped my eyes, wondering why I was so keenly watched by the strange woman. The man ceased his mutterings, and then a third bell was tapped. Every one picked up his knife and fork and began eating. I began crying instead, for by this time I was afraid to venture anything more.

UNITY
DIVERSITY

We've seen that Americans have certain beliefs in common. Are schools supposed to indoctrinate students to create unity? Brainwash them to all know the same things or think the same things?

But this eating by formula was not the hardest trial in that first day. Late in the morning, my friend Judéwin gave me a terrible warning. Judéwin knew a few words of English; and she had overheard the paleface woman talk about cutting our long, heavy hair. Our mothers had taught us that only unskilled warriors who were captured had their hair shingled by the enemy. Among our people, short hair was worn by mourners, and shingled hair by cowards!

PRIVATE WEALTH
COMMON WEALTH

Every culture has different customs and beliefs. How much of our individual lives do we have to give up in order to make a strong common wealth for us all?

We discussed our fate some moments, and when Judéwin said, "We have to submit, because they are strong," I rebelled.

"No, I will not submit! I will struggle first!" I answered.

I watched my chance, and when no one noticed I disappeared. I crept up the stairs as quietly as I could. . . . On my hands and knees I crawled under the bed, and cuddled myself in the dark corner.

From my hiding place I peered out, shuddering with fear whenever I heard footsteps near by. Though in the hall loud voices were calling my name, and I knew that even Judéwin was searching for me, I did not open my mouth to answer. Then the steps were quickened and the voices became excited. The sounds came nearer and nearer. Women and girls entered the room. I held my breath, and watched them open closet doors and peep behind large trunks. Some one threw up the curtains, and the room was filled with sudden light. What caused them to stoop and look under the bed I do not know. I remember being dragged out, though I resisted by kicking and scratching wildly. In spite of myself, I was carried downstairs and tied fast in a chair.

FREEDOM

EQUALITY

Do we have to look the same and act the same to be equal? When should we resist equality and fight to protect our individual freedoms?

I cried aloud, shaking my head all the while until I felt the cold blades of the scissors against my neck, and heard them gnaw off one of my thick braids. Then I lost my spirit. . . . And now my long hair was shingled like a coward's! In my anguish I moaned for my mother, but no one came to comfort me. . . . I was only one of many little animals driven by a herder. . . .

A short time after our arrival we three [girls] were playing in the snowdrifts. We were all still deaf to the English language, excepting Judéwin, who always heard such puzzling things. One morning we learned through her ears that we were forbidden to fall lengthwise in the snow, as we had been doing, to see our own impressions. However, before many hours we had forgotten the order, and were having great sport in the snow, when a shrill voice called us. Looking up, we saw an imperative hand beckoning us into the house. We shook the snow off ourselves, and started toward the woman as slowly as we dared.

Judéwin said: "Now the paleface is angry with us. She is going to punish us for falling into the snow. If she looks straight into your eyes and talks loudly, you must wait until she stops. Then, after a tiny pause, say, 'No.'" The rest of the way we practiced upon the little word "no."

As it happened, Thowin was summoned to judgment first. The door shut behind her with a click.

Judéwin and I stood silently listening at the keyhole. The paleface woman talked in very severe tones. Her words fell from her lips like crackling embers, and her inflection ran up like the small end of a switch. I understood her voice better than the things she was saying. I was certain we had made her very impatient with us. Judéwin heard enough of the words to realize all too late that she had taught us the wrong reply.

"Oh, poor Thowin!" she gasped, as she put both hands over her ears.

Just then I heard Thowin's tremulous answer, "No."

With an angry exclamation, the woman gave her a hard spanking. Then she stopped to say something. Judéwin said it was this: "Are you going to obey my word the next time?"

LAW

ETHICS

Rules are important. But do we just follow rules blindly? Or is it important for our leaders and teachers to help us understand why the rules are important? Did Thowin's teacher do the right thing, the ethical thing?

Thowin answered again with the only word at her command, "No."

This time the woman meant her blows to smart, for the poor frightened girl shrieked at the top of her voice. In the midst of the whipping the blows ceased abruptly, and the woman asked another question: "Are you going to fall in the snow again?"

Thowin gave her bad password another trial. We heard her say feebly, "No! No!" . . .

During the first two or three seasons misunderstandings as ridiculous as this one of the snow episode frequently took place, bringing unjustifiable frights and punishments into our little lives. . . .

The melancholy of those black days has left so long a shadow that it darkens the path of years that have since gone by.

For Zitkala-Sa, education was not about a promising future. It was about loss. By taking away her Indian ways, schooling darkened her future. Many Native Americans reported this same kind of experience.

Schooling took away the culture they had been born to. They lived in a world in which they were not Native American enough to live in their old world and not American enough to be accepted in the modern American world.

There are many levels of common wealth. Yes, our nation—all of us together—build the country's wealth together. But Zitkala-Sa and her people have a culture that is part of their common wealth as well. The common wealths of many different cultures—many different American peoples—combine to make up the common wealth of the United States. It includes Native Americans, southerners, midwesterners, Italian Americans, Asian Americans—the list goes on and on. Each has the common wealth of their original culture. And each culture contributes to the common wealth of our nation. Perhaps to be valuable, education has to help us find our future both as individual people and together as the American people.

CAN EDUCATION WIN THE WAR?

Education is still the future. It's *your* future. And not just your future. It's the future of the whole country. Americans realized that in a big way when the Soviet Union—which was made up of Russia and several Eastern European countries—launched a satellite in 1957.

A new satellite doesn't seem like a big deal in our world. Everybody, governments and private companies, sends up satellites these days. Satellites transmit our television, phone, GPS, Internet, and more. We use satellite services so often we don't even think about the fact that they're up there circling overhead. But in 1957 this was all new.

Even scarier, we were fighting a Cold War against communism, and the communists in Russia were beating us in space.

"Cold War" sounds pretty strange. World War II ended in 1945 when the allies (the United States, Great Britain, and Russia) defeated Germany, Italy, and Japan. But, even though we ended the war as an ally with Russia, our relationship was not good. The term *Cold War* referred to this tension mainly between the United States and Russia.

By 1957 the two countries were facing each other down. Both countries had nuclear weapons. Both were afraid that the other was ready to attack. People believed that a nuclear war was about to happen. So just imagine what it was like when the United States discovered that Russia had launched the first satellite and it was orbiting over the United States. Americans wondered if they were safe. How did Russia get this technology before America? Did it mean that they could drop a bomb on the United States from outer space? Were they using the satellite to spy on Americans? Could America catch up or would Russia control space in the future? In 1957, all across the country, schoolchildren practiced what to do in a nuclear attack. Families built bomb shelters in their backyards. People were scared. Could America survive?

STUDENTS SAVE AMERICA

President Dwight Eisenhower decided that a big part of the solution was education. Americans would beat the Russians at their own game. We would invent more. We would create more. We would not let Russia control outer space. But to be successful, America had to have more scientists.

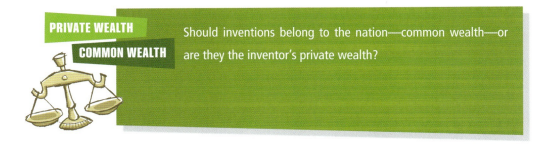

PRIVATE WEALTH / COMMON WEALTH Should inventions belong to the nation—common wealth—or are they the inventor's private wealth?

In 1958, Ike (that's President Eisenhower's nickname) declared that October was National Science Youth Month. Top government officials called for nationwide support of the initiative.

Dr. Howard L. Bevis
Chairman of President Eisenhower's Committee on Scientists and Engineers

"The world was startled with the news that Russia had sent a satellite into orbit. . . . [We must begin the] training of potential scientists or engineers. . . . Preparation of informed citizens of tomorrow, whether or not they ever become scientists or engineers, must begin in junior high school—even senior high school may be too late."

Donald A. Quarles
Deputy Secretary, Department of Defense

"This joint effort of government agencies, professional societies and other major organizations will surely help to promote student interest in the sciences and give every thinking citizen increased awareness of the extent to which our way of life and our national security depend upon continuing progress in this field."

FREEDOM
EQUALITY

Can education really protect the American way of life? What do you think he meant? Are we more free just because we learn about the American "way of life"? Does more education—equal education for more people—make us a stronger nation?

Arthur S. Flemming
Secretary, Department of Health, Education, and Welfare

"National Science Youth Month offers a challenge to citizens and citizens groups to mobilize the resources of schools and communities throughout the Nation in support of science education. It is also a time for all citizens to take stock of the scientific advances . . . [because] the ability to apply this knowledge in an intelligent manner to the great issues of our day, is . . . responsible citizenship."

LAW
ETHICS

Public schools are created by law, and students attend because it is the law. Calling for a National Science Youth Month was an effort to create more scientists and engineers who could help America compete in the Cold War. Is it ethical to use our schools and education as a weapon to win a war?

Leo A. Hoegh
Director, Office of Defense and Civilian Mobilization

"Our future defense will be manned, in very large degree, by men and women trained in science and technology. To meet our civil defense and defense mobilization needs, more and more of our talented young people should seek careers in science and engineering."

BIG TALK DOESN'T MAKE IT EASY.

Getting ahead of Russia wasn't all that easy. They're the ones who sent up the first animal in space (a dog named Laika). Russia was the first to send an unmanned spacecraft to the moon. They were first to take pictures of the dark side of the moon. And in April 1961 a Russian named Yury Gagarin was the first man in space. It didn't seem like America was catching up.

The next month, May 1961, President John F. Kennedy set an audacious goal for Americans when he delivered his State of the Union speech before Congress. "I believe that this nation should commit itself to achieving the goal, before this decade is out, of landing a man on the moon and returning him safely to the earth."

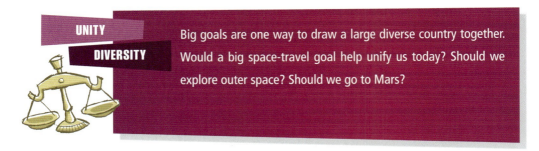

UNITY / DIVERSITY

Big goals are one way to draw a large diverse country together. Would a big space-travel goal help unify us today? Should we explore outer space? Should we go to Mars?

Did Americans really understand how difficult it was going to be? The next year President Kennedy admitted that

> we choose to go to the moon in this decade and do the other things, not because they are easy, but because they are hard, because that goal will serve to organize and measure the best of our energies and skills, because that challenge is one that we are willing to accept, one we are unwilling to postpone, and one which we intend to win.

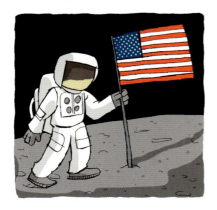

And we did win. In July 1969, the Apollo 11 spacecraft was the first to land a man on the moon and return him safely to earth. The Russian space program never caught up. America used education—our common wealth—to win a major battle in the Cold War.

MORE THAN DOLLARS AND CENTS

There are times when education is a tool we use to benefit all of our community, state, or nation. Education creates common wealth. We can see the common wealth in American citizens using their education to solve communal problems and build strong communities. Common wealth created by education makes it possible to solve big national and international problems, like space travel. Every single citizen has to do his or her part. It's so important to make sure we are always building that strong common wealth.

At the same time, there is no denying that educating our citizens also creates private wealth. Sure, some of that is money. Education opens up a world of job opportunities. But we cannot measure our private wealth just by the size of a bank account. It is more than dollars and cents. Education improves our lives in so many ways. How do you know what freedom and equality are unless you study history about medieval serfs, the Spanish Inquisition, Jim Crow laws, or the Holocaust—times when people were denied freedom and equality? People who work with the law are always studying to understand it better. Lawyers research and study how laws were made and interpreted by the courts over time so that they help and protect their clients. They actually call it "reading the law." People who solve problems have to study and investigate to discover a solution. An engineer, for example, may need to study and test materials to make certain they are strong enough to hold up a building. In all these situations and more, people gain new knowledge. And as they learn, they create private wealth for themselves.

So here's the bad news. You will never stop being schooled. Your whole life will be spent learning. Sure, you will not always have the kind of classroom and teachers you have now. Your classroom might be a place of work. It might be your home. It might be where you worship. It might be a museum or public place. Who knows? But you will always be learning.

THE REAL QUESTION TO ASK YOURSELF IS THIS:

HOW MUCH OF YOUR LEARNING WILL YOU DEDICATE TO YOURSELF—TO YOUR PRIVATE WEALTH—AND HOW MUCH TO OTHERS—TO THE COMMON WEALTH?

American citizens have responsibilities. We are responsible for being the best individuals—the best citizens—we can be. We are responsible for being rich with learning and experiences and all the kinds of private wealth that make for strong individual citizens. But American citizens are also responsible for building strong communities, states, and nation—for building common wealth. And you cannot build a strong common wealth if you're going to be stingy with your education and experiences. How will you contribute? What kind of difference will you make?

WHAT ARE YOUR DREAMS?

Do you have dreams? Things you want to accomplish? Places to go? Things to do? It might seem like those dreams are a long way away. But. Did you know that Benjamin Franklin was only seventeen when he ran away to Philadelphia and started working as a printer? Revolutionary War general the marquis de Lafayette was eighteen when the American Revolution started. Emily Geiger was eighteen when she carried secret messages for the Continental army in South Carolina. Frederick Douglass was not yet fifteen the first time he tried to get his freedom by running away from his owner. Alexander Graham Bell was twelve when he invented his first machine. He would later invent the telephone. Shaun White was skateboarding professionally at age seventeen. Taylor Swift was fourteen when she started her music career. So your dream is not that far away. Are you ready?

People the world over have dreams. But Americans are famous for making dreams come true. Why? Freedom. America has always been a place where people are free to be what they want to be. We call it the American dream. That doesn't mean that it's easy. And it doesn't mean that everyone becomes rich or famous. But in America people have the freedom to try. People have the freedom to follow their own paths. In America, we believe that everyone should have an opportunity to try.

That's the other important thing about the American dream. We believe that dreaming belongs to everyone, that we all have equal opportunity to dream and follow our dreams. And we don't like it when something or some group stands in our way. When Jim Crow laws kept African Americans from pursuing their dreams like every other

American, citizens protested and worked to change those laws. Sometimes change takes a long time, but over and over again Americans have worked to give people equal opportunity to achieve their dreams.

After all, who can say that your freedom to dream is more important than—or less important than—someone else's? As the Declaration of Independence says, every human being is "created equal" and "endowed by their Creator with certain unalienable Rights, that among these are Life, Liberty and the pursuit of Happiness."

IT ALL BEGINS WITH YOU.

Our friend Thomas Jefferson didn't just pull that "Life, Liberty, Happiness" thing out of the air. He didn't make it up. People had been talking about these ideas for a while. It's just that talking about them and making them work are two very different things.

Most places, in Jefferson's day, had very little freedom for everyday people. People believed that God had given the right to rule over others to a small group of people, mostly kings and queens. Everybody else was a "subject" who served a ruler. In this way of thinking, rulers had all the rights. They could, if they wanted, give some rights to everyday people, but only if they wanted to. The people were lucky if they lived someplace where the ruler was generous. The amount of freedom you had depended on what the ruler was willing to give you.

Then new ideas started to come up. It was part of a movement—a new way of thinking—that we call the *Enlightenment*. (We touched on the Enlightenment in the chapter on protesting.) Well, these Enlightenment ideas really took off in America before the Revolution. A lot of people were talking about them and about how to make them work. It was all about individual freedom and equality.

So when Virginians declared independence from Great Britain on May 15, 1776 (you'll notice that's *before* the Declaration of Independence), they decided to write down these Enlightenment principles about freedom and equality. That way, they would know what kind of government they needed to have. They called it the Virginia Declaration of Rights. Their eighteenth-century language can be kind of hard to read, so let's update the language and see just what they said.

We Declare That:

1. People are free. And their freedoms aren't given to them by government. They're born with their freedoms, including life, liberty, happiness, safety, and the right to buy property (stuff) and keep it.

FREEDOM

EQUALITY

So we're all born with freedom. But the guys who wrote this declaration of rights (over two hundred years ago) owned slaves. They believed in their own freedom, but what about the freedom and equality of African Americans? How much equality did they really want the people to have?

2. The people are in charge, not rulers. In fact, rulers, elected officials, and government workers are servants of the people.
3. People give government the right to rule. And government's job is to protect the freedoms of the people. If a government does a bad job, the people can change the government.
4. People are all equal. Nobody gets to be a leader just because mom or dad was a leader. A person has to earn it by being a responsible citizen.
5. Government should be divided so that no one part is too powerful. The executive, legislative, and judicial branches should be separate. And people should not be allowed to stay in office and get too powerful.

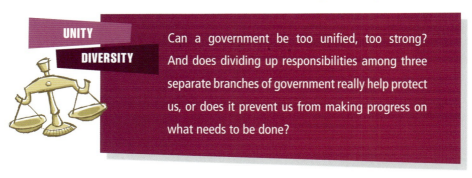

UNITY
DIVERSITY

Can a government be too unified, too strong? And does dividing up responsibilities among three separate branches of government really help protect us, or does it prevent us from making progress on what needs to be done?

6. The country should have free elections, and every responsible member of the community should have the right to vote.
7. The legislative branch directly represents the people, so the legislature is the only branch that can make laws and decide how laws should be enforced.

8. Anyone accused of a crime has the right to face the people who accuse him or her of the crime. The accused also has the right to a trial by jury. And the law can't just lock someone up and say, "Oh, he's waiting for trial." Everyone has a right to a speedy trial.

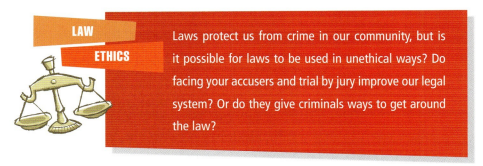

LAW
ETHICS

Laws protect us from crime in our community, but is it possible for laws to be used in unethical ways? Do facing your accusers and trial by jury improve our legal system? Or do they give criminals ways to get around the law?

9. The government can't slap someone convicted of a crime with an unreasonable fine or some cruel and unusual punishment.
10. The government can't just show up and search someone's house or take property without first showing evidence that the person might have committed a crime.
11. If neighbors have an argument over property (maybe over borrowed tools or where the property line is), either neighbor can ask a jury of their peers to decide.
12. Freedom of the press is important. People need to see all the news and talk openly about how government is working. And it's good for the press

to criticize how government works. It helps keep everybody honest.

13. Citizens should serve in the military to defend the community. And when the danger is over, they should return to their civilian lives. The military should be loyal to the citizens and the protection of freedom. They should not be used to keep rulers in power.
14. Government has to be fair.
15. To keep liberty—American freedoms—citizens must work at being educated, just, moderate, understanding, and willing to talk with each other honestly about important issues.

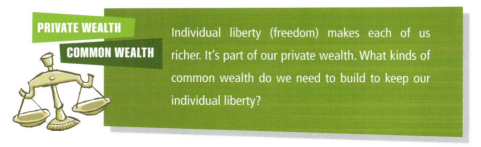

PRIVATE WEALTH
COMMON WEALTH
Individual liberty (freedom) makes each of us richer. It's part of our private wealth. What kinds of common wealth do we need to build to keep our individual liberty?

16. A person's religion is private business. Government shouldn't support one religion over another.

Remember that people were talking about these ideas in the year 1776. Men wrote the Virginia Declaration of Rights. There were no women in the room. And all of the men were white. They did not include Native Americans, African Americans, or any other groups as part of this conversation. They owned slaves. We can point a finger at them today and say that they did not live up to their own ideals. That's true. But it's not just about whether these guys in 1776 lived up to these ideals. Can *we* live up to these ideals?

These are big ideas. They promise a lot—freedom and equality. And living up to these ideals was and is hard. After all, citizens work every single day to improve the world they live in. And American citizens work hard every day to make sure that we protect our freedoms and that every American has equal opportunity to take advantage of those freedoms.

How many ways do citizens work to protect freedom? How many ways do citizens work to encourage equality? We certainly think about the people who serve in our military as protecting freedom and equality. And other public servants are like that—or should be like that. The fire safety and emergency workers in our communities protect our freedoms, our property, and our lives. That's the job of our police officers too. It is also why our communities are so upset and disappointed when police officers are accused of treating citizens unequally. Teachers help protect our freedom and equality by teaching us how to be good, informed, and engaged citizens. Education is one of the things that can make us more equal.

WHOSE JOB IS IT?

But we don't have to have a special job to protect freedom and equality. Think about the protesters who marched for civil rights. Think about every citizen who said, "Yes, I agree and I support you.

I recognize your civil rights." It might not seem like much, but every person who stepped forward and supported civil rights supported freedom and equality for their communities.

What about the citizens who go to community meetings, talk on social media, and stand up at the local school board or city council to speak in favor of freedom and equality? They are all doing their part to protect America.

The work would be easy if we all agreed. But we don't. All through our history our freedom to do something has bumped against our hope for equality. That's what happened with slavery. Slaveholders said that they had the freedom to own other people as property. And they said they were allowed to do it because the people they wanted to own were not equal to them. We don't believe that today. But those slavery days still hang over our country. Are we treating all people equally yet?

WHOSE FREEDOM IS IT?

Sometimes we want the freedom to do something, but in order to have that freedom we have to take freedom and equality from someone else. Doesn't sound very American, does it? But that's what happened to Native Americans. It started in the 1600s and continued all through our history.

Land was hard to acquire in Europe. Over there, somebody—mostly rich noblemen—owned it all. But in America, it seemed like the land was just waiting to be taken.

Of course the problem was that European Americans did not understand and did not appreciate how Native American people thought of the land. American Indians did not have the same idea about owning things. They didn't mark off boundaries on the land and own it. When Europeans came to America, they immediately began dividing the land up into pieces, making farms, and figuring out who owned which piece of land.

As more and more Europeans came, becoming Americans, more and more people dreamed of owning land. In the early 1800s, white Americans demanded that the government give them all the land east of the Mississippi River. There were thousands and thousands of Native American people living there, but that didn't make any difference. White Americans wanted all of it. It was their American dream.

In May 1830, Congress passed the Indian Removal Act, and President Andrew Jackson signed it into law. The U.S. government was going to force Indian tribes to leave their homes and resettle west of the Mississippi River. Some Native Americans challenged the law in court, but it was no use. European Americans wanted the freedom to move west. And if that interfered with Native Americans' freedom to live on the land of their ancestors, so what. The U.S. Army forced Native peoples to travel beyond the Mississippi on a journey that has been called the Trail of Tears.

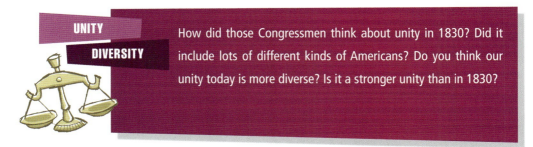

UNITY
DIVERSITY

How did those Congressmen think about unity in 1830? Did it include lots of different kinds of Americans? Do you think our unity today is more diverse? Is it a stronger unity than in 1830?

I WISH I COULD FORGET IT ALL.

It's hard to imagine what it was like, but this story by a man named John Burnett helps us understand how terrible it must have been. John was one of the soldiers ordered to remove the Cherokee people from their land. He was an old man when he wrote this story in a letter to his children. Some historians think he may not have remembered all the details exactly right. But John Burnett did remember how terribly the Cherokee people were treated.

> This is my birthday December the 11th 1890, I am eighty years old today. I was born at Kings Iron Works in Sullivan County, Tennessee, December the 11th, 1810. I grew into manhood fishing in Beaver Creek and roaming through the forest hunting the Deer the wild Boar and the timber Wolf. Often spending weeks at a time in the solitary wilderness with no companions but my rifle, hunting knife, and a small hatchet that I carried in my belt in all of my wilderness wanderings.
>
> On these long hunting trips I met and became acquainted with many of the Cherokee Indians, hunting with them by day and sleeping around their camp fires by night. I learned to speak their language, and they taught me the arts of trailing and building traps and snares. . . .

FREEDOM
EQUALITY

John Burnett grew up with a lot of freedom. Do you think that freedom helped him see Native people as his equals?

The removal of the Cherokee Indians from their life long homes in the year of 1838 found me a young man in the prime of life and a Private soldier in the American Army. Being acquainted with many of the Indians and able to fluently speak their language, I was sent as interpreter into the Smoky Mountain Country in May, 1838, and witnessed the execution of the most brutal order in the History of American Warfare. I saw the helpless Cherokees arrested and dragged from their homes, and driven at bayonet point into the stockades. And in the chill of a drizzling rain on an October morning I saw them loaded like cattle or sheep into six hundred and forty-five wagons and started toward the west.

One can never forget the sadness and solemnity of that morning. Chief John Ross led in prayer and when the bugle sounded and the wagons started rolling many of the children rose to their feet and waved their little hands good-by to their mountain homes, knowing they were leaving them forever. Many of these helpless people did not have blankets and many of them had been driven from home barefooted.

PRIVATE WEALTH
COMMON WEALTH

Government is allowed to take our property for the common good, for example, to build a road that benefits the whole community or to collect taxes to support the services we all need. How can we tell if our private wealth is being used to improve the common wealth appropriately?

On the morning of November the 17th we encountered a terrific sleet and snow storm with freezing temperatures and from that day until we reached the end of the fateful journey on March the 26th, 1839, the sufferings of the Cherokees were awful. The trail of the exiles was a trail of death. They had to sleep in the wagons and on the ground without fire. And I have known as many as twenty-two of them to die in one night of pneumonia due to ill treatment, cold, and exposure....

...School children of today do not know that we are living on lands that were taken from a helpless race at the bayonet point to satisfy the white man's greed....

LAW
ETHICS
The relocation of the Cherokee is something that happened a long time ago. Many people today look back and say it was legal but not right or ethical. Are Americans today responsible for the unethical or illegal things our ancestors did?

Murder is murder and somebody must answer, somebody must explain the streams of blood that flowed in the Indian country in the summer of 1838. Somebody must explain the four-thousand silent graves that mark the trail of the Cherokees to their exile. I wish I could forget it all, but the picture of six-hundred and forty-five wagons lumbering over the frozen ground with their Cargo of suffering humanity still lingers in my memory.

Let the Historian of a future day tell the sad story with its sighs, its tears and dying groans. Let the great Judge of all the earth weigh our actions and reward us according to our work.

Children—Thus ends my promised birthday story. This December the 11th 1890.

European Americans pushed Native Americans farther and farther west and onto reservations because they wanted the freedom to own land. But the freedom to own land meant that Native people lost their freedom to live as part of that land. Is there any equality in that?

Don't think that these are things that just happened in the past. We are still struggling with questions about fairness today. These questions are all around us. How much freedom can I have? How much equality can we have together?

FRESH OFF THE BOAT

How do we decide who gets a chance at the American dream? It isn't open to everyone, you know. People all over the world want to come to the United States because they believe in the American dream. They are searching for a place where they can be free to do things like earn a good living, educate their children, live in a safe environment, and practice their religion. These are powerful dreams. In many places around the world, people are prevented from following these dreams. That's why so many people want to come to the United States. But who will we allow to come?

"We the People"—the citizens of the United States—make decisions about who can come to our country. Often, the decision is based on keeping certain people out. For one reason or another, the American people decide that certain kinds of people are undesirable. That's what happened starting in the 1870s.

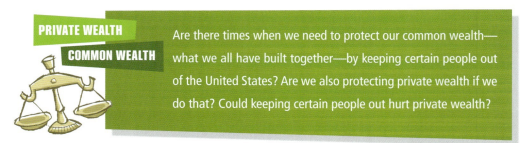

PRIVATE WEALTH
COMMON WEALTH

Are there times when we need to protect our common wealth—what we all have built together—by keeping certain people out of the United States? Are we also protecting private wealth if we do that? Could keeping certain people out hurt private wealth?

After encouraging Chinese laborers to immigrate to California to build the railroads, Americans decided they didn't want the Chinese in the United States anymore. Why? It started with a bad economy. People were out of work on the West Coast, and, once the railroads were completed, it seemed to many Americans that Chinese workers were taking away jobs from American citizens. But, truthfully, it had a lot to do with racism. The Chinese did not look like Europeans. They looked different, dressed differently, spoke different languages, had a different religion—everything about them seemed strange.

Many times, being different is all it takes to make someone—or a whole group of people—outsiders. American citizens began to tell their government that they wanted to keep Chinese people out. And that's what states and the federal government started doing. In 1882, Congress passed the Chinese Exclusion Act. The law tried to prohibit Chinese immigration, but Chinese immigrants continued to come.

So what did this all look like? Here's a political cartoon from 1882 that describes it pretty well.

A—On the North American side of the water, which represents the Pacific Ocean, Americans are building a wall to keep the Chinese out. And the stone blocks are labeled with words like fear, jealousy, anti-low wages, un-American, and competition.

FREEDOM/EQUALITY—
We are often worried someone or something un-American will destroy our freedom. Do you think all of the workers in this cartoon are equal? If the Chinese come, will anyone have to give up freedom for the Chinese to have equality?

B—It's mostly other immigrants who are building the wall. There's an Irishman, an Italian, a Frenchman, an Eastern European, and a Scandinavian. There's also an African American freed from slavery. Now that these people are part of the American dream, they want to keep the Chinese out.

UNITY/DIVERSITY—
Isn't it interesting that all these very different people have united? But is it good that they are united in preventing more diversity? Do you think too much diversity can hurt America's unity? If so, how much would be too much?

CHAPTER 4: THE AMERICAN DREAM 127

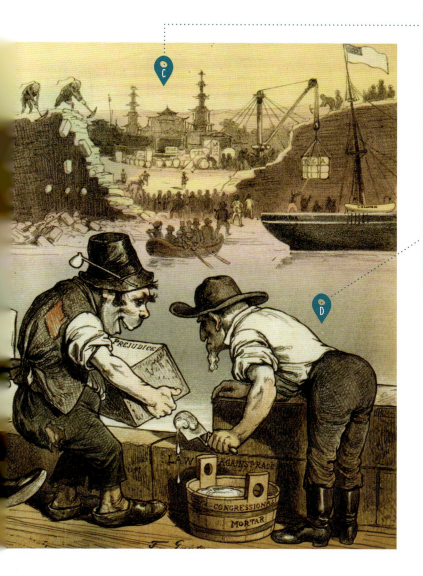

C—China is on the other side of the water, and the Chinese are tearing down a wall. China had blocked trade with America for a long time. Now they were tearing down their trade wall. Americans were happy about that. They wanted Chinese goods, just not Chinese people.

D—The mason building the wall is Uncle Sam, and he's using "Congressional" mortar to lay the stones. What's the congressional mortar? The Chinese Exclusion Act of 1882.

IF THESE WALLS COULD SPEAK

The American dream is a powerful thing. It pulls hard on people. From 1910 to 1940, the U.S. government set up an immigration station on Angel Island in San Francisco Bay, California. Chinese men and women hoping to enter the United States were held there and interrogated.

In 1970, a National Park Service ranger named Alexander Weiss was assigned to Angel Island. The National Park Service planned to open the island as a park. Alexander's job was to get Angel Island ready for thousands of visitors.

The Chinese men and women who had been held in the immigration station on this island had faced terrible racism. Remember, the purpose of the 1882 Chinese Exclusion Act was to keep them out of America. And the hatred against these people was plain to see on

Angel Island. When Chinese immigrants got off the ferry that brought them to the island, the first American they saw was an armed guard. They were herded into a barbed wire–fenced area. They were held for days, weeks, months, and sometimes years.

As Alexander was getting to know the island, he discovered one building that had been the immigration station and barracks for the Chinese. As he looked around, he discovered Chinese characters carved into the walls. The park ranger could not read Chinese, but he sensed that the characters were important. And he was right. But he had a problem. According to the National Park Service plan, the building was going to be torn down.

Alexander began to tell everyone he could about his discovery. A local college professor and the students in his Asian studies class came to see the writings. They started to translate them. They were poetry.

Powerful words about the American dream and what it means to be so close that it is just barely out of reach.

> Instead of remaining a citizen of China,
>   I willingly became an ox.
> I intended to come to America to earn a living.
> The Western styled buildings are lofty; but
>   I have not the luck to live in them.
> How was anyone to know that my dwelling
>   place would be a prison?

Some poets recalled life in China and wondered if they would ever be allowed to return. Others told how painful and discouraging it was to be held on the island like prisoners. Still others wondered if there really was any freedom or justice in America.

> America has power, but not justice.
> In prison, we were victimized as if we
>   were guilty.
> Given no opportunity to explain, it was
>   really brutal.
> I bow my head in reflection but there is
>   nothing I can do.

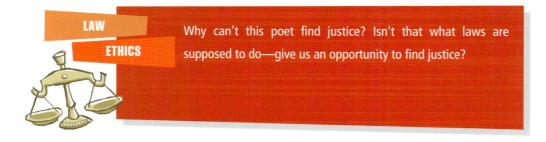

LAW / ETHICS

Why can't this poet find justice? Isn't that what laws are supposed to do—give us an opportunity to find justice?

The U.S. government tried to wipe out this immigrant poetry. Again and again between 1910 and 1940, government workers filled in and painted over the words carved into the walls. But freedom burns brightly in every heart. Each time government workers covered over the poetry on the walls, immigrants carved in new poetry.

Alexander, with the help of friends, students, and teachers, convinced Congress and the National Park Service to save the building and the poetry on its walls. They continue to study the building. Layer by layer historians are uncovering the lives, words, and dreams of the Chinese immigrants who were held at Angel Island.

GOOD PEOPLE OVER HERE—BAD PEOPLE OVER THERE

Americans debate who can come to America all the time. We choose who can follow the American dream. We worry that giving freedom to a new group might mean we have to give up some freedom ourselves. Sometimes we worry that a group of people wants to take away our American dream. Will new immigrants change us or harm us in some way? Or we look at some other group of people and decide that they are not like us. And if they're not like us, can they be equal to us? Americans believe strongly in freedom and equality, so it's hard to think that Americans can actually talk about keeping some people from following their dreams, but it's true. Freedom and equality are big ideas, and living up to those big ideas is hard to do.

A DREAM WORTH PROTECTING

It was hard to believe in the American dream during the Great Depression of the 1930s. Millions of Americans were out of work. People lost homes, farms, jobs, and businesses. Many went without, and for many, everyday life was a struggle.

On top of that, it seemed like the whole world was falling apart. In 1937, Japan invaded China and began spreading their influence across the Pacific. In 1939, Germany invaded Poland and with their Italian allies moved swiftly to control much of Europe and North Africa. The United States entered the war in December 1941 after the Japanese bombed Pearl Harbor, Hawaii. World War II raged in every corner of the globe. No one is sure how many people were killed in this war. It was much more than fifty million men and women.

Nearly every American family had someone serving in the military. Mothers hung blue stars in their front windows to show that their sons and daughters served in the military. And when a service member was killed, the family changed the blue star to a gold star. The soldier's mom was then known as a Gold Star Mother.

Americans worked in the defense industry building weapons, tanks, airplanes, and equipment for American service men and our allies. Children collected scrap metal and essential materials for the war effort. Families farmed victory gardens to increase the nation's food production. Every day people gathered around radios and newspapers to follow the progress of the war. They were hoping and praying it would end soon. In 1945 it did. Americans celebrated. They had won.

CHAPTER 4: THE AMERICAN DREAM 133

WHAT A MESS

When the war was over, the world was a wreck. Across Europe and Asia, whole cities had been destroyed, and millions of people were homeless. North America did not experience that kind of tragedy, but Americans were tired of foreign wars. They looked for a future of peace and happiness at home.

Then the Cold War started. It was a struggle between communism and democracy. It seemed like the Soviet Union and China were spreading communism all over the world. And communism seemed to be saying that people shouldn't waste time on having individual dreams, that people should focus only on what the government decided was best for all the people. Communism was against everything the American dream stood for.

In the United States, Americans reacted to the Cold War by celebrating freedom. It was a time when it was important to celebrate the American dream. And we did. Americans started new businesses, and the economy took off. Americans became leaders in everything from scientific discovery to the arts. Americans bought homes and all kinds of goods. Americans traveled and explored the country and the world. Americans celebrated the American dream.

As "We the People" celebrated, we also went to work on expanding the dream—making sure that every American had equal freedom to be part of the American dream.

Just imagine how you might have described the American dream if you had been in school during the 1950s. Don't you hate it when your teacher hands out those essay assignments? Here's what some of those 1950 essay assignments might have looked like.

Name: Tim Bullock
Date: September 4, 1957

"What does it mean to be an American?"

Mom and Dad took our family to Disneyland this summer. It is wonderful! We drove from San Diego up the Pacific Coast Highway to Anaheim. My little sister's favorite parts were Main Street U.S.A. and Fantasyland. Main Street looks just like the hometowns you see in all those movies. And the entrance to Fantasyland is Sleeping Beauty's castle. My sister liked this best because it's where they have the flying Dumbo and Peter Pan rides.

My favorites, though, were Frontierland and Tomorrowland. Frontierland had the riverboat and the pirate lair on Tom Sawyer Island. It was like going back in American history. But Tomorrowland was really nifty. It was all about the future of America. Just imagine traveling in space and exploring under the sea. They had a house of the future with picture phones. You can actually see the person you're talking with on the phone! And there were remote controls for the television set. Just push a button to change the channels. The kitchen had an oven that cooked food by using radio waves. There was a big clock that showed you what time it was anywhere in the world. And a movie that showed on screens all around you—360 degrees. It felt like you were flying across America.

We had a really boss weekend at Disneyland. It was more than just fun. Like Dad said, Disneyland shows you how great our country is. In Frontierland we learned what a great history our country has. And in Tomorrowland we learned how great the country will become. There is so much possibility for America today. You and I are free to do anything in America!

PRIVATE WEALTH
COMMON WEALTH

The United States is a great country, and the promise of what we can be—our future—is important. But that future doesn't happen just because we celebrate our greatness. We have to build that future together. It takes commitment and sacrifice. What are you willing to give up in order to make our country great?

Name: Julieta Cardenas
Date: September 4, 1957

"What does it mean to be an American?"

My grandmother was born in San Diego. My parents were born here. I was born here. We are Americans and we are proud of it. In America my grandfather and father built a hardware store on Island Street. It's an important business in our community. My family has always been respected and good citizens in the San Diego community. But I was hurt by an experience I had this summer.

UNITY
DIVERSITY

What does it take to be part of American unity? Do you have to be born here? Do you have to make important contributions to the community? How different can we be and still remain one American people?

My family went to the beach. We go many Saturdays during the summer. Madre and Padre with my brothers and sisters. Often we meet my cousins, my primos. There is lots of family to talk to. Lots of other kids to play with. These days are so much fun.

One Saturday in July, my family was at the beach having a wonderful time. We swam and we built a wonderful sand castle. My cousins and I enjoyed the sun and the picnic my madre had packed for us. After lunch, Christina and I took some money we had saved from our summer chores and walked to an ice cream shop nearby. We ordered our ice cream and paid, but just as we were starting to walk back to the beach three Anglo boys started calling us names. They called us spics and beaners and wetbacks. "Go back to Mexico!" the bullies yelled. We were scared and Christina dropped her ice cream. The boys laughed and called us more names. We walked quickly back to the beach and our families.

FREEDOM

EQUALITY

Americans have freedom to speak their minds. But what happened when these boys spoke out? Was there any way these boys could have expressed their opinion freely and still protected Julieta's equality?

Those Anglo boys believe that America is only for them. I do not understand how some people can be this way. I am an American too. It hurts that I must work so much harder than these people to reach my dreams. But I am proud to be an American, and I will succeed no matter how others try to block my way.

Name: Willie Ingram
Date: September 4, 1957

"What does it mean to be an American?"

My father grew up in Alabama. He joined the army when World War II started. Like all patriotic Americans, my father was ready to protect and serve his country. But our country has not always been good to my father. My grandmother was born into slavery. She and my grandfather, my mother and my father have worked hard to get ahead. And it has not been easy. But when the war was over, my father was able to go to the Tuskegee Institute. He graduated with a degree in mechanical engineering. We moved to San Diego so my father could work here. We have a good life in San Diego. Here I feel free to follow my dreams.

This summer, Mom and Dad decided I was old enough to travel by myself and spend two weeks with my grandmother in Alabama. Before I went, though, my father had a long talk with me. He wanted to make sure I understood that things were different in Alabama. Because I am a Negro, I would have to be very careful. Once I got to Alabama, it was easier because I stayed near my grandmother's house. It was a whole Negro neighborhood with stores and churches and everything. But traveling to Alabama was scary. Before I got to Texas, I began to see signs for "whites only" and "colored only." I was very careful to sit in the right section on the train. And I only went to the colored waiting areas in the train stations.

When I got to Alabama, everyone at my grandmother's church was talking about the bus boycott in Montgomery. Negros were only supposed to sit in the back of the buses in Montgomery, so people stopped riding the buses and protested. And if Negros did not pay to ride the buses, the city could not afford to run the bus system. The city's bus drivers and bus mechanics would lose their jobs. They were sure that the city would have to back down and stop segregating the seating on buses. Last summer taught me that every American wants to be free. But being free means that you have to fight for the things that are important to us. Being free is hard work, but in America freedom is more than a dream. We can make freedom and equality possible for everyone.

LAW

ETHICS

Government sometimes charges fees for services, like in this case where people paid a fee to ride the bus. Is it right for people to challenge government this way? Even if it might cost other people their jobs?

During the 1950s, believing in the American dream helped to defend the United States from the threat of communism and the Cold War. Just believing in individual freedom and equality helped everyone to rally behind the country and accomplish some remarkable things. Americans dreamed that all things were possible, and, from popular culture to landing a man on the moon, it seemed that in every way America was better than the Soviet Union and China.

Communism and the Cold War also helped us look closely at the American dream. Sure, we celebrated what was good about America. We celebrated our accomplishments together. It's important to celebrate. That did not mean Americans turned a blind eye to problems. It was also in the 1950s and 1960s that Americans—in large numbers—supported the civil rights movement. We said to ourselves and to the world that freedom and equality were the dream of every individual. More importantly, millions of citizens dedicated themselves to making that dream of civil rights equality a reality for men and women of every race and heritage across the country.

CONCLUSION | # OUR AMERICA

UNFINISHED WORK

The work is not finished. You know that. Just listen to the conversations going on around you at school, at home, and in your community. Americans are still dreaming. We are still dreaming that it's possible to have more individual freedom. We are free to dream about new pathways and new accomplishments. We are still dreaming that it's possible for everyone—no matter what gender, race, age, religion, or personal beliefs—to be the best that we can be. We just want an equal opportunity. The American dream is all about having the chance to be what we want to be.

At the same time, you know there are Americans who have to work harder to realize their dreams. We don't always have equality of opportunity. Sometimes it just isn't fair. The question is, what are you going to do about it?

American citizens work every day to make their dreams come true. No one gives them to them. American dreamers work hard for them. You can choose to work for personal success, to own nice things, and to be an important individual. That's OK. There's no problem with dreaming those kinds of dreams. But American citizens also have a responsibility to make sure that the dream is alive for our fellow citizens as well. We cannot live the American dream alone.

How will you shoulder that responsibility? There are hundreds of ways. Support your school and teachers. Work with programs and organizations in your school to help make sure everyone has the opportunity for a great education. There are groups and organizations in your community that help others achieve their dreams.

The American dream is a powerful thing. It gives us all something to reach for. What are your dreams? What do you want to accomplish? Where do you want to go? What do you want to do? How will you make American freedom and the American dream a reality? How will you support others as they reach for their dreams? It's right here, right now. Anything is possible. It all starts with a dream.

WHAT'S YOUR PLAN?

So we've looked at politicians, protesting, education, and the American dream. You can see how they have each been important throughout our history. Sometimes people get hurt. It's important to remember, though, that if you step back and look at the whole picture, America has become better and better over time.

We have more individual freedoms today than we did in 1776. We have more equality. Our laws are more useful and more ethical. We are a much larger and more unified nation. At the same time, we have so much more diversity today than we did in 1776. And private wealth? America is the richest country in the world. And our nation is a leader in the world because we have created a strong common wealth together.

That doesn't mean that everything is perfect. These American ideals of unity, diversity, private wealth, common wealth, law, ethics, freedom, and equality are really big. There is always more to do. If the United States wants to be the best in all these areas, we will have to keep working at it. We got rid of Jim Crow laws, but that doesn't mean all our laws are ethical. If we are not careful, if we don't work together, if we don't all join in the Great Debate, we can go backward and lose some or all of what we have accomplished in our history.

What are *you* going to do? You will probably have to pick a couple of things that you think are most important to work on. After all, there are hundreds and hundreds of important issues that are part of our Great Debate every single day. You can't weigh in on all of them. Maybe you have a friend with health problems, and the health care system is important to you. Maybe you're part of a minority group in your area, and you're concerned about how the local government and police treat you and your friends. Maybe you or your friends are new to this country, and you are concerned about how immigrants are treated. Maybe you see people who are less fortunate than you and want to help. Maybe you want to dedicate yourself to the defense of our country. Maybe you're concerned about how local government handles its money. Maybe you see something in your community that is unethical, and you want to change it.

The great thing about America is that you get to pick. You can choose how you are going to make a difference. You can work on the things that you are most passionate about. You can change the world.

Just remember, however, that you have to make the commitment. You can commit to make your world better. But, you are also free to be apathetic. You're free to sit home and do nothing. You're free to ignore the people or situations in your community who need help. No one will force you to go out and work on these things. You can choose whether or not to be an active citizen. Being a citizen is not just a right. It's a responsibility.

You don't have to be president, a judge, or a legislator. You just need to join the conversation—the Great Debate. Good citizens are at work everywhere—in families, in schools, in community organizations, in places of worship, in businesses, in government. Everywhere you find people in our country, you find citizens at work. What will you do? How will you take up your responsibilities? How will you join the Great Debate? How will you shape the future of your community, your state, your nation, your world? Anything is possible for the American citizen.

ABOUT THE AUTHOR

William E. (Bill) White is a historian and museum professional. As a fifth grader, he joined the Colonial Williamsburg Fifes and Drums and began a lifelong exploration of museums, American history, civic engagement, and teaching. From 1998 to 2016, he led Colonial Williamsburg's education and media outreach initiative and retired in 2016 as the Royce R. & Kathryn M. Baker Vice President of Productions, Publications, and Learning Ventures. He continues to write, teach, and explore the American experience.

ABOUT THE ILLUSTRATOR

CS Jennings is an illustrator and author who lives in Austin, Texas. He has illustrated over fifteen books, drawn for board and video games, graced the pages of *Highlights* and *Disney Adventures* magazine, and worked on animated movies. When he is not drawing, one of the things he does is study history—so he loved illustrating this book!

ABOUT THE IDEA OF AMERICA™

My America: An Owner's Guide grew out of a standards-based, supplemental, digital program for high school students and adult learners called The Idea of America. The program, which spans American history from precontact to the present, uses multimedia and interactive elements that make primary-source content relevant to today's learners and that encourage active citizenship.

The program was developed by the Colonial Williamsburg Foundation and is distributed by Social Studies School Service. For more information go to socialstudies.com.

Also available is an adult book, *The Idea of America: How Values Shaped Our Republic and Hold the Key to Our Future*, by H. Michael Hartoonian, Richard D. Van Scotter, and William E. White. The book explores core American values and the tensions between them, showing how they have shaped and continue to shape our history.

The book is available from the Colonial Williamsburg Foundation. For more information, go to shop.colonialwilliamsburg.com/The-Idea-of-America.

ABOUT THE COLONIAL WILLIAMSBURG FOUNDATION

Colonial Williamsburg is dedicated to the preservation, restoration, and presentation of eighteenth-century Williamsburg and the study, interpretation, and teaching of America's founding principles. The Foundation operates the 301-acre Historic Area and is the world's largest living history museum. Our mission: To feed the human spirit by sharing America's enduring story.

For more information go to colonialwilliamsburg.com.